Clara's Story

Clara's Story

by Clara Isaacman

as told to Joan Adess Grossman

THE JEWISH PUBLICATION SOCIETY

PHILADELPHIA   JERUSALEM

Library of Congress Cataloging in Publication Data

Isaacman, Clara.
 Clara's story.

Summary: The author describes her own and her family's
experiences during the two and one half years they spent in hiding
in Antwerp, Belgium during World War II.

1. Jews—Belgium—Antwerp—Persecutions—Juvenile literature.
2. Holocaust, Jewish (1939–1945)—Belgium—Antwerp—Personal Naratives—
Juvenile Literature. 3. Isaacman, Clara—Juvenile literature.
4. Antwerp (Belgium)—Ethnic Relations—Juvenile literature.
[1. Isaacman, Clara. 2. Holocaust, Jewish (1939–1945)—Belgium—Antwerp—
Personal narratives. 3. World War, 1939–1945—Jews] I. Grossman,
Joan Adess. II. Title.
Cloth, ISBN 0-8276-0243-X
Paperback, ISBN 0–8276–0506–4
DS135.B42.A575   1984   940.53'15'0392404932[92]   84–14339

Designed by Adrianne Onderdonk Dudden

10 9 8 7 6 5 4 3

The author wishes to thank Rabbi Howard I. Bogot,
Ms. Shirley Green, Mr. Michael Grunberger, Ms. Judy Handelman,
Anneke Knoble, Dr. Rela M. Geffen, Dr. and Mrs. David M. Sklaroff,
Mr. Mitchell E. Panzer, Mr. Daniel C. Cohen, Ms. Pauline Handelman,
Ms. Louise Cohen, Ms. Freeda Brest, Ms. Marcia Trilling Wesler, and
Dr. Gilbert Grossman and his four lovely daughters, Jamie, Karen,
Linda and Suzy for their encouragement and support
in the writing of this book.

This work is dedicated to the memory of my late husband,
Dr. Daniel Isaacman.

Illustrious in deed;
an exemplary teacher

רב המעש; מחנך דגול למופת

Contents

Family Photograph

Some years ago I attended an interfaith conference on the Holocaust where Elie Wiesel was speaking, and my husband, Dr. Daniel Isaacman, president of Gratz College, was the moderator. Today I cannot remember exactly what was said, but I can recall very clearly thinking I could no longer remain silent about my two and a half years in hiding during World War II in Antwerp, Belgium. When World War II began, there were 60,000 Jews living there. They, together with all of Belgium's citizens, took life and freedom for granted. Out of that 60,000, only 5,000 survived. I was one of them.

Many people had risked their lives to save mine. They were not all Jews, but they understood and practiced the ideals that are common to all faiths. They valued human life, regardless of religion or nationality. Some of these brave, selfless people perished in the attempt to save their country and to keep people like me and my family alive.

For many years I found it too difficult to talk about the cruelty and viciousness that I had witnessed or to imagine the horrors I had not seen. After the war, I learned that while I was in hiding, 6 million Jews were killed, nearly 2 million of them children.

Being a teacher and lecturer, I was invited to speak about my experiences to young people of high school and college age. Because of their reaction to my story and their request for more lectures, I decided to dedicate myself to telling the new generations about my experiences.

1 · A visit from Uncle Emil

March 1938

The first hint we children had of any trouble occurred one night at dinner while Uncle Emil, my mother's brother, was visiting from Czechoslovakia. The main course had been cleared away. My brothers and sister and I were scraping the pudding out of our dessert dishes, trying to make it last so that we would not be sent to bed. Daddy and Uncle Emil were talking about politics. I wasn't paying much attention, but suddenly their voices started to get louder. Looking up, I was surprised to see Uncle Emil shaking a warning finger at my father.

"This Hitler is a madman, Sholom," he said. "I know how you feel, with a good business and your family settled. But if Hitler takes over Belgium, your business will be worthless. And as a Jew you'll be in more danger than you were in Romania!"

Of course, everyone knew about Adolf Hitler, chancellor of Germany, and about his anti-Jewish activities.

Lately, I had overheard snatches of quiet conversations between my parents. I had heard the word *Nazis* mentioned, but as soon as my parents realized I was listening, they changed the subject. I hadn't thought too much about it until Uncle Emil started arguing with Daddy.

"I respect your opinion, Emil," Daddy replied in his courteous, quiet manner, "but I feel you are too pessimistic. World opinion will stop Hitler. And we can't run again. Once is enough."

Mama had been listening intently, her eyes moving back and forth between the faces of the two men she loved most in the world. As if making a decision, she turned to Uncle Emil. "It won't happen here," she announced with a firm nod.

"Well," Uncle Emil said. "I wish you would change your mind. Look at me. I left Romania, too, but I'm moving again. This time to Palestine. Everything's going, even my furniture factory. You should come, too!"

With these words, Uncle Emil spread his arms wide, as though to gather all of us at the table under his protective wings. For a moment, I thought Mama looked doubtful. But then a private look passed between her and Daddy, and her face became resolute once more.

"We are staying, Emil," she said firmly. "We wish you good fortune and a safe journey."

I couldn't bear to hear my parents arguing with Uncle Emil. He came to see us so rarely, only every two or three years. It made me feel awful to hear them disagree. Just a few hours ago we had been so excited and happy. Uncle Emil had arrived with gifts for everyone. He laughed and joked as he unpacked his bags.

"Well, little one, and what do you think I have for you?" he asked me teasingly, holding a small thin package just out of my reach.

"You don't have to bring me anything," I protested.

"Go ahead, Clara, open it," Frieda urged as Uncle Emil handed me the beautifully wrapped package.

I gasped as I opened the box. There, on a piece of black

velvet, was a beautiful Swiss watch. I had never had a watch of my own. Somehow, Uncle Emil had known exactly what I wanted. It was the same with Frieda and Heshie and Elie. For Frieda there was a gorgeous necklace; for Heshie, a wonderful pocket knife with different kinds of blades and even a tiny pair of scissors. Uncle Emil gave Elie a leather-bound copy of the stories of Victor Hugo—in French. A book may seem like a strange present for a young boy, but Elie already liked books better than toys. There were presents for Mama and Daddy, too, and laughter and stories about growing up together in Romania.

But now, when the discussion turned to leaving Belgium, everyone's mood had changed. Just the thought of leaving Antwerp seemed impossible.

We all knew the story of how Mama and Daddy had left Romania. Daddy was beaten on the way to vote in a local election. The local citizens did not want Jews to vote. When Daddy came home, bruised and angry, he decided that we were moving out of Romania.

My only memory of Romania was of my grandmother, Mama's mother, and the gold watch that hung around her neck. I could remember sitting in her lap and playing with the watch, but, as hard as I tried, I could not remember anything else.

When we moved to Antwerp in 1932, we were young. Daddy set up a soda-bottling plant in back of our house on Leeuwerick Street, where Mama often helped him and the hired men pack heavy lead-topped glass bottles into wooden cases. The bottles were filled with soda water and were then sent all over Antwerp.

At the time of Uncle Emil's visit, we had been living in Belgium for almost nine years. Mama and Daddy often told us how lucky we were to be growing up in Belgium, where Jews were treated just like everyone else. We went to school with other Belgian children, and Mama and Daddy had many Belgian friends.

As Frieda and I cleared the table, Mama, Daddy, and

Uncle Emil started reminiscing. Hearing them laugh over an old story, I felt everything was going to be all right. Surely Uncle Emil was wrong about our being in danger because of Adolf Hitler.

Later, lying in bed, I could hear the grownups talking late into the night. Could we be in danger from Hitler's Nazis? Were Mama and Daddy really sure of their decision to stay in Belgium? Life was so good, so secure for us in Antwerp. How could anything bad happen to us here? What did Uncle Emil know that we didn't?

But I was not the sort of person to stay awake worrying about things I could not control. Speaking sternly to myself, I said, "Mama and Daddy always know what to do. Everything will turn out fine." And with this in mind I fell asleep.

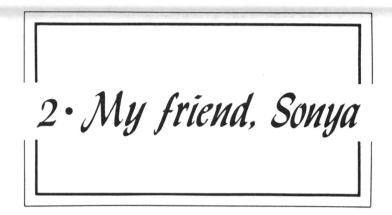

2 · My friend, Sonya

October 1938

Sonya passed a note to me while our teacher, Miss Van Heuten, was writing on the blackboard. I didn't want to get in trouble. I held the note in my hand for a long time without unfolding it while Miss Van Heuten talked about recent events in eastern Europe. When she walked over to the map, I quietly unfolded Sonya's note. It said, "Let's go to the candy store right after school." Honestly! Sonya was my best friend, but she could be really foolish at times. Imagine risking detention for that!

I gave Sonya a wink which said that I'd love to go. Then I turned my attention back to Miss Van Heuten.

"Who can summarize for the class what has happened in Europe during the last six months?"

I raised my hand. Since Uncle Emil's visit, our family had discussed Hitler and his Nazi party almost every night at dinner.

"Well," I began, quickly standing to the right of my desk, "last March, Hitler took over Austria. This was against the rules of the peace agreement of 1919. Then, just last month, September twenty-ninth, I think, Germany took over part of Czechoslovakia."

"Good, Clara," Miss Van Heuten said as I sat down again. "What was Hitler's reason for taking this part of Czechoslovakia?" she asked.

One of the boys stood and explained that Hitler claimed that the Sudetenland, a part of Czechoslovakia where a lot of German-speaking people lived, should be part of Germany. Someone else mentioned that the British and French heads of government had a meeting with their counterparts in Germany and Italy. There they decided on the fate of the Sudetenland without allowing anyone from Czechoslovakia to attend the meeting!

My mind wandered back to that dinner with Uncle Emil and his warnings about Hitler. That was only six months ago. I wondered whether Mama and Daddy thought about Uncle Emil's advice to leave Belgium. If they did, they didn't tell us about it.

I didn't have time to worry about politics. I was busy trying to do well in school. Then there was Hebrew school in the afternoons and my youth group on the weekends. In Hebrew school we learned Bible and history. In my youth group, Hashomer Hatzair, we learned about Palestine. We spent our weekends and much of the summer hiking and camping, learning about the pioneers who were making the desert bloom. Many of my youth-group friends hoped to make *aliyah*—that is, emigrate to Palestine. I wasn't sure I would ever want to live that far away from home, but I loved learning about the land and what our people were accomplishing. I loved the songs and the dancing. Soon I would be skilled enough to be a leader and teach younger children what I had learned.

Life was very full then. I had just spent a wonderful summer at Hashomer Hatzair camp. I really felt like a Belgian. I was very much at home in the beautiful countryside just outside of Antwerp, and this feeling was strengthened when Sonya, a native Belgian, would visit me at camp and take part in our activities. No wonder, then, that Sonya and I became inseparable when school resumed—studying, playing, shopping, and sometimes even going together on hikes sponsored by Hashomer Hatzair.

But, while I was busy studying and playing, Hitler and his soldiers were busy, too. In March 1939 the Nazis occupied the rest of Czechoslovakia. The following September, German soldiers invaded Poland. Two days later, Britain and France declared war on Germany.

Everyone talked about the war. There were neighbors in our house almost every night discussing, over endless cups of coffee, every possibility.

Daddy always brought strangers home from the synagogue on Friday night for Sabbath dinner. There were businessmen from out of town, rabbis visiting Antwerp, and even traveling salesmen. Sometimes they told amusing stories or had interesting adventures to relate. But now, more and more, they talked about what they had heard and seen of the Nazis in other parts of Europe. They talked about the fighting in Poland, how Germany and Russia had agreed to divide that country between them. They told us about sporadic fighting along the French border, and wondered whether Hitler would be stopped before he would make any movement toward the west.

At first, Hitler said he wanted only what rightfully belonged to Germany. This was his reason for taking over Austria, Czechoslovakia, and Poland. But on the morning of April 9, 1940, the Nazis invaded Denmark and Norway. It was clear to everyone that Hitler could not be believed.

If Denmark and Norway were vulnerable, what about Belgium? Belgium is one of the lowland countries lying between Germany and the North Sea. For centuries, it was considered the battleground of Europe. On their way to battle, armies marched through Belgium, never around it.

Now Belgium had declared itself neutral, and Hitler promised that he would, eventually, sign an agreement respecting that neutrality.

We gathered around the radio every night to listen to news of the fighting to the north. Somehow, it all seemed so far away. We still didn't feel that anything could happen to us, to the country we lived in.

3 · The Invasion

May 1940

The Germans invaded Belgium in May 1940. There was much confusion during those early days of the invasion. Many neighbors came to our house to discuss what to do next.

We could hear the bombs going off in the distance. I remember thinking, "How close those bombs sound. Could this really be happening? Is my Belgium really being attacked?" As I served coffee in the living room during a lull in the bombing, I had a chance to listen to the adults talking.

"I'm taking all my money out of the bank and going to Switzerland as soon as this quiets down," one of the men said.

"Don't be in such a rush," replied another. This was a man who often walked to synagogue with Daddy. "You know the Allies will force the Germans back inside their own borders. It's just a matter of sitting it out."

"While we're sitting it out, we may be getting ourselves killed!" Mrs. Markowitz told her husband.

"What do you want *me* to do?" he asked her.

All he got for an answer was an impatient shrug from his wife. I knew that they were too poor to leave and that Mrs. Markowitz had great, unfulfilled ambitions for her shy, studious husband who tried to eke out a living as a diamond cutter. I felt guilty about the plans our family was making, wishing that, somehow, we could take everyone with us who wanted to come.

Daddy was convinced that the Nazis were bombing only military installations and strategic locations. Antwerp is built on the Scheldt River. It is the third largest port in Europe. The country that controls Antwerp, Daddy explained, controls all the shipping and supply routes to and from the North Sea. That is why Germany felt she needed our city. Daddy believed that the Allies—that is, France and England—would defeat Germany quickly. But, in his cautious way, he was making plans to go to France as soon as possible. And from France, we daydreamed, we might go to England or even the United States. If only the awful shelling would stop!

At night the city huddled under an orange, smoke-filled sky. Warehouses along the docks had been hit and were on fire. The screams of sirens filled the evening air as fire fighters rushed about trying to contain the flames. On the outskirts of the city, Belgian soldiers were fighting to drive back the Nazi invaders.

Feeling safer together, several neighbors slept at our house during the week of the bombing. Mama comforted everyone and organized meals. At the same time, she and Daddy insisted that life would go on as usual in a few days, so we studied and made plans almost as if it were a normal week.

Frieda's youth group was scheduled to leave on a camping trip Friday morning, May 17. Frieda was upstairs packing while the rest of us gathered around the radio in the living room to hear the latest news.

"Citizens of Antwerp," began the familiar voice of the local radio announcer, "do not be alarmed."

Mama and Daddy gave each other a quick look.

"We are being liberated by the army of the Third Reich. For your own safety, all residents of Antwerp are requested to remain at home for twenty-four hours until the change of authority is completed. I repeat, for your own safety, everyone must stay home."

The announcement was repeated over and over again. What did it mean, we asked each other.

"'Liberated'" exlaimed Heshie. "That's a funny way to put it. Liberated from what? Freedom?"

"There's no point in getting angry, Heshie," Daddy said. "Let's wait and see what happens. We'll be ready to leave as soon as the curfew is over."

The handful of neighbors who had spent the night at our house prepared to go home to wait out the curfew and make their plans.

"Clara," Mama said softly, "please go and tell Frieda to start unpacking. There won't be any camping trip."

So, I thought as I walked upstairs, Belgium has been defeated. Belgium's earnest efforts to preserve its neutrality had come to this. In just a week since the initial invasion on May 10, Belgium had fallen.

"Frieda . . . " I began as I entered her room.

"We lost, Clara, didn't we?" she muttered. "I can't believe it really happend. What are we going to do?"

"Don't worry," I said in a voice more confident than I felt. "Mama and Daddy will know what to do."

That afternoon, I went down to the train station to see several of our youth leaders off. They were on their way to Switzerland—the one country able to maintain its neutrality—where they hoped they would be safe. There was hugging and tearful good-bys at the station.

I lingered at the station after the train was gone, for I had been told, quietly and in secret, that Pita, the president of

Hashomer Hatzair for all of Antwerp, was also leaving, but on a later train. When the few of us who were seeing Pita off finally found him, we were surprised to see him in street clothes. Before, he had always worn his Hashomer Hatzair uniform.

He just nodded at us and motioned for us to sit down and act as if we didn't know him. He spoke to us only when he was sure no one was looking, and then only in a whisper. He told us that he was not going to Switzerland, but had made connections with the illegal Youth Aliyah—the underground system that since 1932 had been smuggling young Jews into Palestine.

We were not to mention any of this to anyone; we were not to say good-by to Pita before leaving the train; we were not to wave as the train pulled away.

It was only because of my pleading that Pita allowed me to take a picture of him, as I had of the other leaders earlier. Then, again, maybe it was only to keep me quiet; Pita's eyes darted about suspiciously before and after the quick, uneasy smile he flashed at the camera.

Then, without a word, we rose one by one, nodded, and muttered good-by in the general direction of Pita, who simply sat and stared out the window. It was not until I was walking down the platform, listening to the train pulling away behind me, that I realized my youth-group leaders were riding on a train through occupied Belgium, wearing Zionist youth-group uniforms.

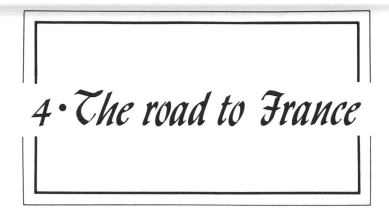

4 · The road to France

May 1940

At 6:30 the following morning, May 18, 1940, we listened as
the radio announcer described the scene at Antwerp's town
hall. Two German army motorcyclists presented themselves
to the mayor, who formally surrendered the city to the
invading army.

Our family had been busy during the twenty-four-hour
curfew, packing clothes and valuables in preparation for our
trip to France. After listening to the announcement, Heshie
and Daddy loaded all the valises into the car. When the trunk
was full, they crammed the remaining packages onto the
floor of the back seat.

At 8:00 A.M., when the curfew was officially over, we
piled into the car, each of us loaded down with valuable items
we couldn't leave behind. It felt so strange to be saying good-
by to our house, leaving furniture and dishes, and so many
precious memories behind. Mama said we would send for our
belongings after we found a place to live. She and Daddy had
arranged with a neighbor to ship everything to us.

Mama and Daddy sat in the front seat with Elie between them. Heshie, Frieda, and I shared the back, our legs straining for space among the bundles and suitcases. Mama had packed lunch. We planned to have dinner in France.

This is a real adventure, I thought, as Daddy started the car and turned into the street. It was a beautiful spring day, and I looked forward to the drive through the countryside and then into France. I had never been to France, and, even though I knew the French were at war with Germany, I was still anxious to see their country. We studied French as well as Flemish at school, and I loved learning about French culture and reading French authors. Yes, it was strange to be leaving home, but it was exciting nevertheless.

Daddy made good progress until we neared the out-skirts of the city. There, vehicles of every description were jockeying their way onto the main road that headed southwest toward the French border.

"I guess we weren't the only ones with this idea," Frieda said.

"You're right," replied Daddy. "No one wants to wait around to see what it's like to live under Nazi occupation!"

It was impossible to do anything but inch forward on the crowded road. What was normally a drive of just a few hours stretched into an entire day. The drinks and sandwiches disappeared at midday. By the time we neared the French border, it was already getting dark and we were all tired and edgy.

"We're almost there, children," Mama said. "Just be patient a little while longer."

Elie dozed off in the front seat. Heshie, Frieda, and I craned our necks trying to catch a first glimpse of France. Something strange was happening a little way up the road. Ahead of us, the cars reached a certain point and then turned around.

"What's going on over there?" Daddy asked the driver of a car coming back.

"You can't cross the border," came the reply. "The Germans have closed off all the roads into France."

It was true! As we rode closer, we saw German soldiers holding rifles, leaning into cars, and giving instructions. A young blond trooper signaled us to stop. In polite German, he told Daddy that all roads in northern France were now controlled by the German army.

"Please turn your car around, sir," he said with a patient air. "It's perfectly safe. Go home. Nothing will happen to you."

There was silence in our car as the young man walked past us to the next automobile. None of us had actually expected to come in contact with a German soldier. I think we were surprised by his courteous manner and the matter-of-fact way in which he told us to return to Antwerp.

Elie, roused from his nap by the sound of the soldier's voice, was the first to speak.

"What will we do now, Daddy?" he asked. "Can we go home, Mama?"

Mama smiled as if to say she wished going home were as easy as he made it sound.

The traffic seemed to move even more slowly than before. Twilight thickened into darkness, and we saw other weary families stopping by the side of the road, eating supper or stretching out on blankets to wait for the traffic to ease up. In the front seat, Mama and Daddy spoke in low tones, weighing our choices now that we couldn't get to France. What else could we do but go home? Nothing, they decided. However, there seemed little point in spending the night traveling slowly back to Antwerp. We were all tired and hungry. What we needed was a place to stay.

Daddy turned the car onto a side road and drove until we saw the lights of a farmhouse. Soon we were standing in the middle of an old kitchen, more primitive than any room I had ever seen. There was a stone floor and white-washed stucco walls, where pots encrusted with years of cooking hung on pegs. A huge fireplace filled one wall. Against the opposite wall stood a large wooden table with thick legs and a plain wooden bench on either side.

Daddy offered to pay the farmer and his wife in return for supper and a place for us to sleep. The couple was happy to earn some extra money, and quickly accepted Daddy's offer.

Mama asked, "Where may we wash up for dinner?"

"Wash?" the woman asked. "Why would you wash now?"

"It is our custom," Mama replied quietly.

The woman directed us outside to the water pump. Heshie pumped water for all of us to rub our hands under, then I pumped for him. There was no soap.

I walked back into the kitchen ahead of the others, thinking I could help the woman with supper.

As I laid the plates and forks on the table, I could see the farmer's wife looking at me, a bit puzzled. "Tell me, child," she finally asked. "Tell me, if Jews are supposed to be so dirty, who do you wash so much?"

I was so shocked by her question, I didn't know whether to laugh or cry. Clearly, the woman had never seen a Jew before. Smiling to myself, I wondered what she had expected Jews to look like. Horned, probably—like Michelangelo's sculpture of Moses. Or hook-nosed and filthy, the way some of the German-language newspapers pictured us.

Despite her comment, the woman and her husband were gracious hosts. After dinner, Frieda, Elie, Heshie, and I settled down on the kitchen floor on straw-filled sacks. Mama and Daddy slept on sofas in another room. What a strange day, I thought to myself before I dozed off. We left our home, met a German soldier, and were called dirty Jews! And tomorrow we're going back to Antwerp! It was all too strange.

The next morning, after a big country breakfast of porridge and homemade bread, we said good-by to our hosts and headed back to Antwerp. There was much less traffic than the night before, and by lunchtime we were entering the city. As we got closer to Antwerp we saw more and more German soldiers traveling on foot and in trucks. We were struck by how young they looked and by how polite and helpful they were, whether directing traffic or waving at us from the backs of their canvas-covered transports. This thing called *occupation* doesn't seem so bad, I thought.

The house was as we had left it. Mama and Daddy had been afraid it would be vandalized as soon as we were gone, but everything was in place. The house felt comfortable and familiar, and I was secretly glad to be back.

But Daddy was not reassured by the friendliness of the Nazi soldiers and the security of being in our own home once more. He and Mama began almost immediately to plan another escape from Belgium.

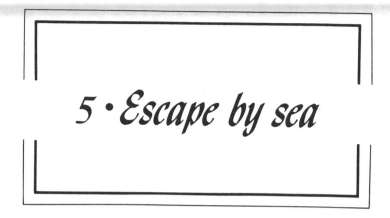

5 · Escape by sea

June 2, 1940

"What are we going to do?" Elie asked for the hundredth time that week.

Daddy looked at him in that special way that said "Not now, Elie" and, reaching for the bread, murmured the blessing to begin the meal.

"Amen," we all said.

"Well?" Elie persisted, "Are we going to run away again?"

Daddy could not resist a grin.

"Since you put it so frankly, yes, we are planning to leave Belgium."

"But Daddy," Frieda objected, "yesterday's newspaper said we shouldn't go."

"And that's what makes our decision so difficult," Daddy said.

We had all read the newspaper article the day before. General von Falkenhausen, the German commander in chief for Belgium and northern France, was quoted as saying, "There will be no action taken against Belgians who thought they had to flee to France. . . . I hope . . . to see the swift return of the Jews of Antwerp, whose presence is necessary for the functioning of the diamond industry."

The article had gone on to explain that the Jewish community in Belgium was small and, therefore, different from Jewish communities in eastern Europe. The Nazis had no intention of rounding up Belgium's Jews and confining them in special areas—concentration camps—as they had in other countries.

"Can we believe what they say, Daddy?" Heshie asked. "Why would they treat western European Jews any differently from eastern European Jews?"

"I wish I had the answer to that question, Heshie," Daddy said, shaking his head. "I wonder if they said the same things to Jews in Czechoslovakia and Poland before they forced them to live in ghettos."

"In the *Jewish News*, the *Judenrat* tells Jews to avoid trouble by obeying every Nazi regulation," Frieda said. "If it's all right to stay, why are so many people running away?"

"Daddy and I feel that the safest thing is to leave, Mama said. "We can't be sure what will happen here, no matter how the Nazis reassure us."

On May 28, 1940, just ten days after we had tried to escape to France, King Leopold III of Belgium surrendered the Belgian army to Germany. Daddy said it was time to leave Belgium.

His plan was for us to drive to Ostend, the home of Belgium's fishing fleet and our favorite seaside resort. Ostend is only sixty miles west of Antwerp. From there, my parents had heard, we could board a ship to England, which lies just west of Belgium across a narrow strip of the North Sea.

Daddy needed several days to put his business affairs in order. We packed the car once more and, on the morning of

Friday, June 2, 1940, we set out for Ostend. This time we brought no trunks with us, only suitcases packed with clothes and a few precious items, such as my mother's Sabbath candlesticks, our seder plate, and our menorah. We had vacationed at Ostend in past summers, and, as we got under way, I could picture the pebbly beach, Mama and Daddy on bicycles, my brothers and sister and me at the amusement arcade. I looked forward to seeing the little seaside town again.

Nearing the main highway heading west, we realized that it was going to be as difficult to go to Ostend as it had been to go to France. Once again, the roads were jammed with people. I wondered whether they had been crowded every day since the invasion or only since the king had surrendered.

Sometime in mid-afternoon our car ran out of gas. Daddy walked to the nearest farmhouse to see if he could buy enough gas to get to Ostend. He didn't even consider trying to reach a gas station. The nearest one was miles away, and the traffic made the idea of getting a ride there and back impossible.

There was no gas at the farm, but Daddy arranged for us to have a meal there while we discussed what we were going to do. We sat down in the kitchen to a table laden with homemade bread and butter, milk, and fruit. We ate and talked with great emotion, while the farmer and his wife sat calmly by, listening and wondering what we were running from.

Mama and Daddy weighed our choices while we ate. Reason told us that it would be terribly difficult to reach Ostend without a car, but we had come so far and no one wanted to go back. We could abandon our belongings and walk, one of us suggested, but the others refused. We had left our home and our friends. We were not going to give up what little we had managed to save. Finally, the farmer insisted that we take his horse and wagon.

Daddy maneuvered the horse and wagon into the stream of traffic on the road, and we walked the fifteen miles that lay between us and Ostend. We took turns leading the horse and walking behind the wagon, afraid to ride for fear the animal would tire before we reached our destination. All around us were masses of people, some in cars, some with pushcarts, others wheeling baby carriages. The crowd had almost a holiday air about it. Occasionally, convoys of British and Belgian soldiers passed us. These troops had been defending Belgium when the king surrendered to Germany. Because the German army had taken control of the roads in northern France, these soldiers were isolated from the main body of Allied forces to the south. They, too, were trying to escape to the sea. Every so often, to our amusement, we passed a British truck parked by the side of the road, with soldiers sitting underneath, sipping tea. Seeing the soldiers enjoying their traditional afternoon tea was somehow reassuring. They certainly don't look worried, I thought, and I felt better about our chances of getting to England.

Walking in western Belgium is not difficult. The terrain is flat, crisscrossed by rivers and canals. Dikes hold the water back from flooding the land. The soil is rich, and we passed one farm after another, their neatly plowed fields already green with rows of peas and beans ripening for market. In the meadows cows grazed lazily, seldom bothering to glance at the strange parade on the road. However, children left their chores or games to wave and stare at us. Adults, too, gaped at us with open-mouthed curiosity.

Summer evenings are long in Belgium. The sky stays light until almost ten o'clock. We walked until nine and then looked for a place to stop. A kind family agreed to give us supper and let us sleep in their barn. We slept on sweet hay and awoke early in the morning to barnyard sounds. It took me a minute or two to remember where I was and what had happened the day before. My feet were so swollen from all the walking that Daddy had to make slits in my shoes so that I could get them on. After breakfast in the farmhouse we harnessed the horse to the wagon and started off once more. Soon my feet became so uncomfortable that I took my shoes off and walked in my stocking feet.

As we approached Ostend, we became aware that the Germans were trying to prevent the Allied soldiers from escaping. First we saw planes and smoke in the distance. Heshie said that there must be an air battle going on. As we watched, a plane fell from the sky and dove, nose first, into the horizon. Dear God, I thought, there are men on that plane! How strange this all seemed. The countryside was so peaceful, and in the distance men were dying.

At the edge of town the scene began to change. There was evidence of bombing everywhere. Huge holes were torn open in the road and in the fields. Several houses looked like they had been worked on by a haphazard wrecking crew. Where a bomb had hit, walls were torn away, leaving rooms exposed. Chandeliers swung at crazy angles; chairs and tables teetered precariously on the edge of the remains of a floor. Where were the people? Had anyone been hurt? None of us asked these questions out loud. We already knew the answers.

As we got closer to the water, we saw bombs falling into the ocean. There would be a loud "boom," then water spurting up from the sea like a fountain. In the center of town were houses that had gone up in flames when they were hit. Some were nothing more than smoldering heaps of wood and stones resting on charred remains. The pretty seaside resort I had known as a child was almost unrecognizable.

In the streets, the holiday air of the crowd changed to panic. The bombing, which had been sporadic and distant, was now very close. Every few minutes, planes bore down on the town and dropped their deadly cargo. The crowd pressed toward the docks. Daddy left us with the wagon and went on ahead to try to make arrangements for our passage. We sat down to wait in the shade of a building across from the wharf where we could watch for Daddy. The noise and confusion swirling around me made my head swim.

"It won't be long now, " Mama reassured us gently.

Leaning back against the building, I closed my eyes for a few minutes, trying to imagine how lovely it would be at sea, the waves lapping at the boat, carrying us to a new life.

"I can't believe it," Mama was whispering, almost sobbing.

My eyes flew open. I must have dozed for a minute. There was Daddy, looking terribly upset.

"What happened?" I asked, shaking myself awake.

"Shh!" Heshie whispered, nudging me with an elbow and nodding toward Daddy.

Thoughout all this—all the traveling and packing and planning—Daddy had been like a rock. But now, I almost did not recognize him. For the first time he really looked afraid.

Daddy started speaking, his voice so choked with emotion that I had to lean forward to hear him.

"When I got to the shipping office, the people in charge told me that the last ship had already left the docks. There will be no more boats leaving for England—the bombing has made it too dangerous. It's no use. We have to go back to Antwerp. Everyone is being turned away."

Wordlessly, wearily, we turned the horse back the way we had come. One hour, I thought; if we had gotten there just one hour earlier we would be on our way to England now. On the other hand, I argued with myself, if we were on the ocean now, we would make an easy target for those bombers. Through a haze of disappointment I thought, maybe this is for the best.

All around us were other people, looking just as disappointed. Before we reached the outskirts of Ostend, low-flying German planes began a concentrated bombing of the town and harbor. People started running, frantic to get out of Ostend.

Since western Belgium is flat and treeless, except for

the poplars that grow alongside the canals, we could watch the bombers approaching. When a plane was headed directly toward us, we dove for shelter as fast as we could. We huddled in hallways and stores, or pressed against the side of a building for protection. As one plane approached, a huge knot of people rushed into a hotel that had a bomb-shelter sign posted outside the door. We started to join the crowd, but Mama shouted, "No, this way!" and we followed her to the other side of the street where we lay down on a porch. The plane droned overhead. Then there was an explosion. When we looked out at the street, we gasped. The hotel was gone.

There was no time to think about the horror we had just witnessed. We scurried off the porch and got the horse and wagon under way again. Walking along a canal, we heard planes approaching. Three men standing on a bridge in front of us started waving and shouting to us.

"Get down! Get down!" they screamed.

In all the confusion, we hadn't noticed a plane bearing down on us from behind. I leaped toward the canal and lay down, burying my head under my arms. Frieda jumped in beside me.

The next thing I was aware of was Mama crying, "Clara, are you all right? Help! Clara's been hit! Clara's bleeding!"

I must have passed out for a few minutes, because I couldn't remember what had happened. A bomb had fallen about half a block away. A piece of shrapnel spinning out of the explosion had pierced my back near my left shoulder blade. I didn't feel any pain. I tried to tell Mama that I was all right, that we should keep going, but she and Daddy were steering me here and there, asking people where to find a first-aid station.

We were directed to a summer cottage that smelled of medicine. People were sitting in the living room waiting to be cared for. Many were wounded, others had twisted ankles running from the bombing. We could hear the strafing still going on, but it didn't seem so threatening inside the house.

A nurse called Mama and me into the kitchen. There was no doctor, but a priest was administering first aid.

"Ach, little one," he said, looking at my back, "it's nothing. A scratch! Just a few stitches and you'll be as good as new."

"Stitches! I don't want stitches," I cried, suddenly afraid.

"You won't feel anything," he reassured me. "Just sit still and it will be over in a few minutes. This way you won't have an ugly scar."

Mama held my hand, and the priest worked quickly, just as he had promised. I only felt little tugs as he patched the tear.

Outside again, we found that Daddy had let the horse free in a field. The poor animal was hard to control with all the noise and excitement, and we had not been able to feed or give him water since the night before.

"He was so tired," Daddy said, "I didn't have the heart to ask him to pull any more."

We took turns pushing and pulling the wagon toward Antwerp. Once we were well outside Ostend the bombing stopped.

In the late afternoon we began to see convoys of German soldiers heading toward Antwerp. They clearly felt themselves in charge. They marched with confidence, singing victory songs. I hated their swagger, but I was too tired from the long hours of walking to pay them much attention. My feet were cracked and swollen. We were all exhausted, hungry, and thirsty, and the wagon seemed to get heavier and heavier. All I could think about was how we would ever make it home with all our luggage. I started daydreaming, planning what we could leave by the side of the road. While I was mentally unpacking the bags, Daddy was paying attention to what was happening on the highway.

"Look," he said.

There was a row of trucks a short distance away. German soldiers had "borrowed" the vehicles in Antwerp, and they were picking up some of the weary people who were returning, like us, on foot. Mama and Daddy looked at each other. Shall we try to get a ride, their look said, or do you think this is a trap? We had heard that German soldiers in eastern Europe had carried Jews away to concentration camps on the pretext of helping them. Soon one of the open-backed trucks pulled alongside our pitiful little group.

"Come up," a soldier called with a smile. "We'll take you home. Don't worry, you'll be perfectly safe."

Other people were already sitting on the benches on either side of the van. Caution seemed foolish in the face of so much comfort. Daddy smiled at us for the first time that day, and we all helped throw our luggage into the center of the truck bed. By unspoken agreement, the adults sat on the benches and the children perched on the luggage in the middle.

When we were ready to start, another German soldier approached our truck and asked the driver for a ride. The truck was full, so the soldier joined us in the back. Before climbing aboard he pointed his rifle, its bayonet fixed, at all of us.

"There'd better not be any Jews here. I won't ride with Jews!"

No one spoke. We didn't even look at each other. After a second's hesitation, he climbed aboard. The adults squeezed over to give him room. We rode in silence, but after a few minutes the soldier riding with us suddenly started to sing the song of the Brown Shirts, as Hitler's troops were called:

Crush the skulls of the Jewish pack
And then the future it is ours and won;
Proud waves the flag in the wind
When swords with Jewish blood will run.

I felt chills run up and down my spine in spite of the warm afternoon sun. This is like a bad dream, I thought. The walking, the horse, the bombing, people screaming and running, the suddenly dead bodies all seemed too strange and horrible to be real. Is this really happening to me?

Then all at once we were home, delivered like packages to the doorstep by our well-mannered enemy. How delicious to bathe away the dirt of our journey and sleep in clean beds.

Now we had no choice. We would find out firsthand what it was like to live under Nazi occupation.

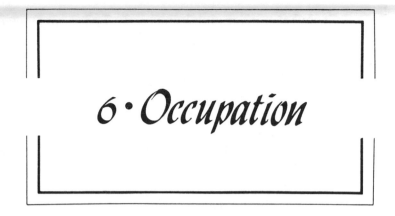

6 · Occupation

October 1940

There was no more talk of escape at our dinner table. We settled back into our lives in Antwerp and watched and listened for the effects the Nazi occupation would have. The summer passed uneventfully. Frieda and I went camping once again with Hashomer Hatzair. We sang Israeli songs and talked about Palestine. Frieda continued her voice lessons. Heshie was learning to make jewelry. At the end of the summer he gave me a silver Mogen David, a Star of David, that I wore proudly on a chain around my neck from that day on.

In September, school opened as usual. We went to the public school on Lamonier Street every weekday and attended Hebrew school three afternoons a week in the old building on Takhkimoni Street. No one paid much attention to the occupation during those early months; we lived as we always had. Even the most skeptical among Mama's and Daddy's friends were lulled by the Nazis' behavior, and the conversations in our living room had a more hopeful tone than it had before we had run to Ostend.

"It might not be so bad to sit the war out here in Antwerp," one of Daddy's friends commented one evening over coffee and cake.

"We're lucky things worked out this way," said another. "If we had succeeded in running away, we would have lost everything—our houses, our businesses. We would probably be in a strange place right now learning a new language!"

All the people who had gathered at our house during the warm fall evenings seemed to feel the war would be over soon; we had only to wait.

But our sense of security was short-lived. In October, the Nazis shocked the Jewish community by issuing "regulations." Jews were forbidden to hold government positions, to practice law, to teach at public schools or universities, to write for or manage newspapers or radio stations. Between October 28 and December 31, 1940, every Jew whose work brought him in contact with the Belgian public was removed from his position.

This made sense, I heard the adults say, as they tried to find logical reasons for each new restriction. Of course, after the way the Nazis had dealt with Jews in their own country and in eastern Europe, they wouldn't want Jews in positions where they could alarm a radio audience or a group of university students.

In May 1941 Jews were forbidden to attend public gatherings. No more than five Jews could congregate in one place. It never occurred to me that such regulations would affect our family, but I arrived home from school one afternoon to find Mama pacing in the kitchen, staring at a piece of paper in her hands.

"What's the matter?" I asked.

"Your father has received a summons," she said, holding the paper close to my face with trembling hands.

"He is charged with playing cards in the middle of a busy intersection. He must report to police headquarters within twenty-four hours."

"That's ridiculous!" I protested. "Daddy would never do such a thing! He'll explain it all to the police."

"No!" said Mama with determination, "I don't think that's the way to handle it."

By the time Daddy came home, Mama was even more certain that Daddy should not report to the authorities. We were all sitting around the table in the kitchen; no one was interested in dinner.

"But Sholom," she insisted as Daddy tried to reason with her, "you know Jews have been beaten by the Gestapo at the police station!"

With these words her hand flew to her mouth, and she looked at us anxiously. I knew she and Daddy had tried to prevent our hearing about such incidents. Daddy shrugged his shoulders as if to say we would have to find out eventually. Mama grabbed the summons from the table and tore it into tiny pieces. We all gasped.

"There," Mama said flatly, throwing the pieces into the garbage pail. "It never came."

Signs started to appear in the windows and on the outside walls of stores and restaurants that were owned by Jews. "JUDE" they said in large red letters. Some of the signs surprised us. The local stationery store across from our school, for example, where we bought paper and ink, was owned by a sweet old man who we never realized was Jewish. He was indignant that the Nazis could force him to put the embarrassing sign in his display window.

"Eh, Monsieur," I overheard him say challengingly to one of his customers while I was choosing some school supplies. "How is it that you still come to my store? Aren't you afraid the Nazis will see that you have dealings with Jews?"

"Ach, Monsieur Dryden," the customer replied, "you

and I have been doing business all these years. You don't think those Nazi scare tactics will keep me away, do you? I don't care whether a man is Jewish or not. If he's honest, he gets my business. Besides, I would have to go halfway across town to find another store with merchandise of this quality. Let's forget such foolishness!"

But the foolishness was not forgotten. Nazi propaganda on the radio, in the newspapers, and on posters all over town encouraged all Belgians to stay away from Jewish businesses. Many Jews soon found themselves in financial difficulty. Shops began to close.

"Why are they doing this?" people asked. "This is bad for the economy."

"It's just temporary," said some. "The Nazis are flexing their muscles, like neighborhood bullies with a group of younger children."

The summer of 1941 passed. Now, however, my youth-group discussions changed from political theory to practical talk about plans to hike to Switzerland and, from there, make our way to Palestine.

"You'll do no such thing," Mama said when I told her, her dark eyes flashing angrily. "I want you children here with me and Daddy. The war will be over soon, and everything will return to normal."

"Yes, Mama," I agreed, secretly disappointed that I would not be part of the exciting planning that was going on.

The Nazis announced that Jewish children would not be allowed to attend public school after December 31, 1941. On that last day I tried to memorize every detail of my classroom: the neat rows of desks, the maps high on the walls, the blackboard behind Mrs. Neibauer's desk, the windows on my left overlooking the front entrance. I studied my classmates through a shimmer of unspilled tears. All morning I had tried to catch Sonya's eye, but she never turned my way. Why was she behaving like this on our last day in school together?

Mrs. Neibauer passed out a piece of paper.

"This is for your parents, children," she said seriously. "You may read it. But read it quickly and then put it away. And make sure it gets home safely."

It described the Resistance, an organization of Christians and Jews that was working quietly against the Nazi occupation. "Christians and Jews of Antwerp," it began, "do not submit to the forces of oppression and discrimination without a fight." The paper went on to describe how all citizens could help to frustrate Nazi objectives. We all knew that it was illegal to distribute such information.

Mrs. Neibauer stood at the window looking out at Lamonier Street while we read. All at once she uttered a tiny cry. Looking up, I saw that her face had turned ashen.

"Students," she said in a strained voice as she turned to face us, "there are some Nazi army officers walking up the front stairs. We are going to be visited. Please do as I say, and don't ask any questions."

We looked at one another and at the incriminating paper.

"Boys and girls," she continued in a voice that trembled only slightly, "each of you must tear that paper into small pieces and eat it as quickly as you can."

We all knew the seriousness of the situation. For the next few minutes the only sound in the room was that of paper being torn, chewed, and swallowed. Everyone did as he or she had been told. My heart was thump-thumping so strongly I was afraid I wouldn't be able to swallow.

By the time the visitors made their way to our classroom, everyone was busily writing a composition about the winter holidays. Mrs. Neibauer greeted the officers in flawless German and asked if there was anything they would particularly like to see.

"*Nein*," answered a tall officer wearing glasses. "We would just like to look around."

"We are honored," said our teacher with a smile.

The men passed up and down the rows of desks for a few minutes, chatting with a few students, leafing through almost every notebook, as though this were the most ordinary activity for Nazi army personnel.

They must have known about the paper, I realized. But how? Would anyone betray Mrs. Neibauer? My pulse raced wildly as hands reached across my desk for my notebook. He knows I'm Jewish, I thought in panic. He knows about the paper! What will they do to us? How can Mrs. Neibauer joke and chatter like that?

Then it was over. Our teacher nodded and bowed as she ushered the last officer out the door. The class continued as though nothing had happened. No one mentioned the paper again.

As the Jewish children left school that afternoon for the last time, Mrs. Neibauer solemnly shook each student's hand. I felt extra warmth in her smile as she said, "Good-by, Clara. I hope to see you again soon."

I turned and ran down the hall, hoping to catch up with Sonya so that we could stop at the candy store on the way home. But she hadn't waited for me. She was nowhere in sight.

"That's odd!" I said aloud, more annoyed than angry. "What's the matter with *her*?"

Often Mama and Daddy talked late into the night about what was happening to the Jews of Antwerp, to the Jews of Europe . . . to us. From snatches of conversation I had overheard, I knew they were trying to make sure we would have enough money to live no matter what happened. Jews could no longer withdraw their money from the bank. We knew that we would never see that money again. My parents also knew they would have to find ways of hiding money.

Antwerp is one of the largest diamond centers in the world, and almost everyone is involved in trading diamonds. Like many of Antwerp's residents, Daddy did a small amount of trading at the diamond exchange, buying and selling precious stones. One night he called us into the living room after dinner.

"I want everyone to watch what I am going to do," he said.

Using a hammer and a screwdriver, he carefully removed a section of the door frame at the entrance to the room. Then he drew a folded piece of white paper from his jacket pocket. He unfolded the paper to show us the diamonds. After a moment, he refolded it, placed it in the hole he had made, and, without saying a word, replaced the door frame so perfectly that no one would suspect it had been touched.

"Children," he said finally, "I am putting the diamonds in here just as a precaution. Chances are we will never have to take them out. But just in case we need them, it's important that you all know where they are."

Then Daddy put his hand in his pocket once more and took out a diamond ring, set with one large stone. He handed it over to me.

"If you ever need to buy your way out of a difficult situation," he explained gravely, his voice now barely above a whisper, "if you ever, God forbid, need to sell something in order to live, that's what this ring is for. Please God, you will never have to use it."

This was a drastic precaution. We had by then lived under German occupation for nearly two years, and things had become steadily worse for Jews. No one wanted to admit that all the Nazi promises about the regulations being temporary were just empty words. As the list of our inconveniences, humiliations, and deprivations lengthened, we started to believe the horrifying reports smuggled out of eastern Europe.

I had tried to visit Sonya, but she made it clear that we were not to be friends any more. I had run to her house to share some new books. Out of breath, I bounded up the steps and knocked loudly. My best friend opened the door a crack. I could hardly see her.

"Go away, Clara," she whispered. "Go away! I'm not allowed to be with you any more."

"Are you joking, Sonya?" I asked, trying to ignore the sinking feeling in my stomach.

"No, Clara. Please, please go away," she begged, tears gathering in her voice.

"Why?" I demanded, I knew the answer, but I needed to hear her say it.

Her voice was even quieter than before as she whispered, "You are a Jew!" and closed the door.

I backed down the stairs slowly. Had I heard correctly? Standing on the pavement for a long moment, I stared up at the house where we had shared so many secrets and happy times. Then I turned and ran, tears streaming down my cheeks.

My sobs were coming in short gasps as I ran the three blocks home. Rushing headlong through the house, I burst into the kitchen and out the back door to the factory where I knew I would find Mama. I needed to feel her arms around me.

"Sha, sha, Clara," Mama murmured, stroking my hair and guiding me outside again, away from the workers who were filling the lead-topped soda bottles and packing them into wooden cases. "Calm down, my dear," she said quietly in Yiddish, leading me back to the kitchen. "Sit down. I'll give you some tea, and you'll tell me what happened."

When I finished telling her my story, she said, "Those are frightened people. They have been listening to the horrible propaganda the Germans have been broadcasting on the radio and writing in the newspapers. Soon things will return to normal. You'll see."

Mama spoke confidently, nodding her head and tapping the table with a forefinger to emphasize her conviction.

Later, when the nightmare was finally over, I would remember that morning as the beginning of our long slide into fear and horror, and wonder whether Mama ever really believed her own reassuring words.

New restrictions were placed on Jews every week now, usually accompanied by violence. Stores were looted and destroyed by mobs. Our synagogue was burned down while police and firemen, under Nazi orders not to interfere, stood by and watched.

Our family endured some private harassment. Nazi soldiers had learned about our soda factory and, as the weather became warmer, they would often enter our house uninvited and order us to run out back and fetch them bottles of soda. Then they would sit in the kitchen drinking and joking, trying to scare us with talk of what happened to people who didn't cooperate.

One evening four of these "guests" were drinking soda in our kitchen, some sitting, some leaning against the wall. Mama, Frieda, and I were clearing away the supper dishes. Suddenly, the lights went out, followed by the distinct sound of a rifle bolt sliding into firing position.

"I'll shoot," barked one of the soldiers.

No one moved.

"If the lights are not turned on at once, I'll fire this gun."

"Excuse me," Mama said in a low, cool voice, "I believe one of you has leaned against the light switch. If you will feel the wall in back of you, you can turn it on yourself."

We laughed after the soldiers had gone, but it was laughter tinged with fear.

In May, the Nazis issued orders requiring young Jewish men to go to labor camps. Their families were promised that no other members of the family would be taken. To boys like Heshie, any kind of work seemed preferable to the enforced inactivity imposed by the restrictions of the occupation. Jewish children could not go to school; they could not participate in organized sports; even their social life was curtailed because of the rules against large gatherings. Jewish boys by the hundreds signed up for the labor camps and were taken away.

Heshie wanted to go, too. For days, all our family talked about was whether he should go, whether the Nazis could be trusted to keep their word, whether he would be safe. Mama and Daddy tried to talk him out of going; they no longer believed in Nazi promises. But, in the end, Heshie insisted on deciding for himself.

"I will feel that I am helping you," he told Mama the night before he left. She sat quietly, dabbing at her eyes with a handkerchief.

Heshie left after breakfast the next morning.

"See you in a few weeks," he called back to us as he walked away jauntily, carrying his suitcase.

The next week we received a postcard. He was fine, he wrote, and really looking forward to having some work to do.

We never heard from him again.

After Heshie left, new rules were imposed almost every day. We had to wear a yellow Star of David on our clothing whenever we went out. Jews were forbidden to practice medicine or to dispense drugs. There was a curfew; Jews had to stay inside their homes between seven in the evening and seven in the morning. All Jews in Belgium were required to live in the large towns of Brussels, Antwerp, Liège, and Charleroi. We were not permitted to sit in trolleys and buses. We were forbidden to go to public movie houses, theaters, or sporting events.

One afternoon, without telling my family, I skipped Hebrew school to go to a birthday party. When I got home from the party, our house was in an uproar. Mama was crying. Daddy was pacing the floor. Neighbors were sobbing, clinging to one another. When Mama noticed me standing in the doorway staring at them in bewilderment, she gave a shriek and rushed toward me.

"Clara, Clara," was all she and Daddy could say as they embraced me. Little by little, everyone told me his or her version of what had happened that afternoon. A German army truck had been parked across the entrance to my Hebrew school. All the teachers and children inside the school were herded into the truck and driven away. I didn't question the quirk of fate that had kept me away. I could only think, I should have been there. Where were my friends now? Where were they going? Would the teachers look after them? How would I have behaved had I been with them?

The incident at my Hebrew school showed us the true face of the beast that was bearing down on us. But it was too late. Every known avenue of escape had been closed. We were trapped.

7 · Candles flickering in the dark

Friday, July 22, 1942

Our curtains had been closed at sunset in compliance with the
blackout laws. There could be no light that might help guide
a British airplane seeking to bomb Antwerp. If the curtains
had been open even a crack, we would have noticed the
torches lighting up Leeuwerick Street as though it were noon
on a summer day. Instead, the first thing that disturbed the
quiet of that Sabbath evening was the sound of heavy
German army trucks stopping at both ends of our block.
They had to be army trucks, I thought, because it was well
after curfew, when only Nazi soldiers were allowed to be on
the streets.

Next I heard the stomping of boots marching on the
cobblestones. Even after two years of occupation, the sound
of Nazi soldiers marching sent a shiver of terror through me.
Curiosity overcame my fears, and I rose from the dinner
table to see what was going on. Daddy turned off the lights,
leaving the Sabbath candles flickering behind us in the

darkness. We followed Mama into the dark living room where she drew the blackout curtain back from the window just enough to let us see out.

On each side of the street stood Nazi soldiers holding flaming torches. Huge trucks were parked at either end, crosswise, blocking all entrance to and exit from our block. The houses on Leeuwerick Street were all connected to one another, so that unless someone would have climbed over a back garden wall, everyone living on our block was trapped. Like helpless animals in a cage, all we could do was wait. In silence, we returned to the table.

We hadn't long to wait. We heard the first screams almost immediately. Soldiers were going from house to house, knocking on doors, demanding to see the passports and identity papers that everyone in Belgium was required to carry. After a brief glance at the documents, the soldiers ordered everyone in the house aboard the waiting trucks. We could hardly believe that the worst, the most unbelievable of the rumors we had heard from eastern Europe, was taking place right outside our front door. The soldiers were herding people into trucks—the young and the aged, the healthy and the crippled—making no attempt to keep families together. Our neighbors were being dragged, shoved, pushed onto those trucks. When someone refused to answer their knock, the soldiers would quickly break down the door. I could hear people pleading and crying, their voices interrupted by the rough commands of the soldiers, sometimes followed by the thud of a rifle butt striking an unprotected head. We sat in stunned silence, listening as the soldiers moved from house to house, waiting for the inevitable, unbearable moment when it would be our turn. The voices were growing more frantic.

"Malka, where's my baby Malka?" Mrs. Lefkowitz's terrified voice rose in a screech.

Mama gripped the edge of the table.

"She's in a truck," came the gruff reply.

I remembered, little Malka was sleeping at a friend's

house that night. She was probably in a truck with her friend's family.

"Which truck, which truck?" shrieked Mrs. Lefkowitz.

Then we couldn't distinguish Mrs. Lefkowitz's screams from those of the others.

"Be careful!" someone shouted just outside our door. "Can't you see she's in a wheelchair? She can't walk!"

Dear God, I thought, that must be Perele, our crippled neighbor. Everyone loved her. She was young and full of life in spite of her illness.

"Be merciful," begged another neighbor, a male voice this time.

"They're dragging her by the hair! Oh, my God, my God, help us!"

We were next.

"Passports!" demanded the two soldiers who suddenly filled our front hall with a blur of uniforms and guns.

We all gathered around Daddy, determined to stay together.

Calmly, slowly, Daddy handed over our passport folders. When had he put them in his jacket pocket, I wondered. We held our breath as the soldier leafed through one folder after another.

"Romanian?" he barked.

"Yes," Daddy replied.

"Everyone?"

"Yes. My whole family."

"We are not taking Romanians or Belgians," he said. Germany and Romania were allies. The Nazis were evidently under orders not to offend Romanian citizens. But the Nazi officer knew we were Jews; he stared angrily at the Sabbath candles that flickered on the table.

"Is there anyone else in this house?" he asked. My parents just looked at him. Surely he knew about the Chaimowitz family. It was just a week ago that soldiers came and took Mr. Chaimowitz away. They had pushed him down the stairs and dragged him out the door by his beard. Were the Nazis testing us?

There was silence for a moment. Then my mother nodded at me and asked me to show the soldier upstairs. As I started to climb the stairs, the soldier motioned to my parents to wait. He then cocked his rifle and pointed it at my head the entire way up to the third floor.

As I climbed those stairs, I wondered why that rifle was pointed at me. I had done nothing. I was not a thief or a soldier. I was only a Jew.

What am I doing, I thought, I am taking this Nazi to a Jewish family.

At the top of the stairs was the door to the Chaimowitz's room. The door was open slightly, and a little light shone from inside into the hallway. I stood and listened to the breathing of the Nazi soldier behind me.

"Open," he ordered. I opened the door, and there was Mrs. Chaimowitz sitting on the bed, her twelve-year-old son, Shloimeh, standing rigidly at her side. The soldier nudged me into the room.

"Is this the whole family?" he asked Mrs. Chaimowitz. She looked directly at him and nodded. My eyes flitted around the room. Where was Batya? She must be hiding.

The soldier turned to me. "Is this the whole family?" he asked. I nodded, knowing full well that if he had only *walked* around the room, he would hear Batya breathing. And if he did find her, my entire family would be taken with Mrs. Chaimowitz.

"All right, let's go!" he ordered. We marched out of the room and down the stairs. My parents were waiting there. I could see them looking at Mrs. Chaimowitz and Shloimeh and wondering what happened to Batya. The soldiers followed Mrs. Chaimowitz and her son out the door without another word.

As they left, Daddy closed the door and we were alone again. The noises in the street began to die down. We heard the trucks start up and slowly drive away.

After a few quiet minutes, Daddy opened the front door a crack and we peered outside. Our beautiful street seemed to echo with the cries of those who had been taken away. Here and there on the cobblestones were pools of blood. Perele's wheelchair lay on its side in the gutter. Favorite toys and bits of clothing were strewn about in the street. All was quiet now. But it wasn't the restful quiet of the Sabbath. It was the hushed quiet of death. Daddy closed the door. A chill came over me, as though a damp November fog had settled around our house, making me invisible to the rest of the people in the city, leaving me alone in what was suddenly unfamiliar territory.

"It's too dangerous for us to live here any longer," Daddy said. "I think we are the only Jews left on Leeuwerick Street. Today they are not taking Romanians. Tomorrow they may change their minds."

"Go children, put some things together," Mama instructed us, "but not too much. It must not look like we're moving."

"Where are we going?" Elie asked.

"We'll see," Daddy answered patiently. "Someone is sure to come looking for us. The whole city must have heard what went on here."

"Go ahead, children," Mama urged. "Try to get some sleep."

Somehow, in the confusion, no one had thought to look for Batya, hidden on the third floor. Now, as we left the dining room, we were shocked to see her sitting quietly on the bottom step, her eyes wide with fright. She was a beautiful little girl, dressed for the Sabbath. Mama scooped the child into her lap, holding her close and murmuring words of comfort. We all tried to talk to her, but she could only nod her head in response to our questions. Reluctantly, we went upstairs and got ready for bed, leaving Mama and Daddy to make plans for us all.

What should I take with me, I wondered. I looked around my room. Dolls and books filled the shelves;

mementos cluttered the bureau and the night table. What did I absolutely have to have? I remembered the silk tablecloth tucked away in a bottom drawer that Daddy had given me, telling me to put it away for my marriage. It was the custom, he explained, for eastern European Jews to buy their daughters beautiful things to use when they were married. Daddy had given me the cloth to use in a future I could not imagine. I folded it into a small square and set it on my bureau.

What else was absolutely essential? My glance fell on the photograph album sitting on my bookshelf. I had spent so many pleasant hours sorting and pasting pictures of my friends, my family, and my youth group in that album. I could easily carry it under my arm. And, of course, I would wear the watch Uncle Emil had given me on his last visit.

It was almost impossible to sleep that night. It seemed as though I had just dropped off when I felt Mama shaking me awake, whispering that I must get ready quickly. Someone from the Resistance was coming to take us to a hiding place.

"What about Batya?" I wanted to know.

"She's fine," Mama replied. "The Resistance is taking care of her, too."

The people in the Resistance had been working secretly against the Nazis. I could still taste the paper I had eaten on that last day of school that explained what the Resistance— or Underground, as some called it—was all about. Now the Resistance was helping us, too. I thought about the night before with a shiver as I put on as many layers of underwear, blouses, and skirts as I could.

At the bottom of my drawer I found a small case and in it the Star of David Heshie had given me for my last birth-day, with the word "Zion" engraved on one side and "Clara" on the other. I wished that Heshie was still with us; we'd be stronger with him. I quickly put the necklace around my neck.

When everyone was ready, we climbed upstairs and

onto the roof to see what the neighborhood looked like in daylight. There was a deathly quiet hanging over the street. Nothing moved. Windows were open here and there, flowerpots overturned on the sills. Had people tried to escape out their windows? Or had they decided to accelerate the timetable the Nazis had in mind for them and jump to their deaths? The more I looked, the more certain I became that we were the only family left on Leeuwerick Street.

At 6:00 A.M. a bland-looking man, Mr. Yeager, Frieda's music teacher, came quietly through the kitchen door.

"Is everyone ready?" he whispered.

We nodded yes. Mr. Yeager explained that we would stay in the basement of Ballotin's bakery on the next street until a better place could be found.

"You must walk normally," he told us, "in twos and threes, as though you're going to visit friends. Try not to attract any attention. Above all, if you see Nazi soldiers, ignore them completely and keep walking."

Trembling inside, I whispered a furtive good-by to the house I loved and stepped into the street with my family. We started down the deserted road. We were only four houses from the intersection of Leeuwerick Street and Sommer Street. There we had to turn left at the butcher store and walk half a block to the bakery. The distance ahead seemed to grow longer with each step.

Elie and Mama walked in front with Mr. Yeager. My little brother's curly dark head bobbed from side to side looking for the enemy in this deadly game of hide and seek. Daddy, Freida and I walked a short way behind them, each of us clutching our most precious possessions. The bundle that Daddy carried was a crumpled paper bag no bigger than mine. I knew that in it were his tallith and tefillin—the prayer shawl and phylacteries that he used during his daily prayers—and his prayer book.

What if we are stopped by a soldier, I wondered, and he demands to see what is in Daddy's bag? We would certainly be arrested. Just as I was thinking this, Daddy reached down with his free hand and tucked something into my collar. My silver Star of David had come out from under my coat. I was horrified to realize that we had been walking through the streets with a Star of David plainly in view. I looked up at Daddy. He must have seen fright and tears in my eyes. He just smiled reassuringly and nodded, "It's all right."

As we reached the corner we all slowed down. Once we turned left we would be exposed along the entire length of Sommer Street. I had no doubt that we would be shot if we were seen coming out of Leeuwerick Street. I held my breath as Mama and Elie walked around the corner with Mr. Yeager. Nothing. I looked left and right. Sommer Street was empty.

Mr. Yeager wordlessly hurried us along the sidewalk, past several gaping front doors, to the bakery. He led us beyond the store entrance into a narrow hall and down a flight of stairs that turned at the bottom. We found ourselves in a large room under the bakery. There was no furniture, only sacks of flour stacked in the corners. A window high in the wall let in a little light.

"You'll be safe here if you are absolutely quiet," Mr. Yeager assured us. "We are looking for a more comfortable place for you to stay."

Then he was gone, leaving us to make the best of our strange surroundings. Keeping away from the window, we arranged a few flour sacks so that we could sit.

We whispered, "What next?" "How long do we have to wait?" "What if the soldiers find us?" "Are there other people hiding?"

"Children, children," Daddy said, "enough questions. This is a new situation for your Mama and me. We will all have to be patient for a little while and have faith in the good people of this city. Mr. Yeager has already taken a great risk just bringing us here. We must be grateful for his help and trust that he will find us a better place as soon as he can."

The day passed slowly. We had been set adrift on unfamiliar waters. Suddenly everything I knew was gone. Only my family existed for certain, and, in another sense, we didn't exist at all. As far as we could tell, no one but Mr. Yeager knew where we were, knew even that we were alive. I could only guess about what had happened to our neighbors. As we sat there in the dim basement light, our conversation turned from our personal problems to questions about the situation of all European Jews.

We wondered if there were any Jews left. How could such a thing have happened? How was it possible, we would ask Daddy, that an entire country like Germany could hate the Jews with such a hatred?

"We are the scapegoats," Daddy explained. "Since the world war of 1914, the German people have sacrificed and suffered. They have paid dearly for losing that war. Their people are tired of rationing and shortages, of inflation that made their money worthless."

"Hitler is clever," Mama said. "He tells the people that all their troubles are caused by the Jews. According to him, Jews have taken advantage of Germany's kindness toward them and are preventing her real citizens, those of 'pure Aryan descent,' from realizing their proper inheritance."

"Hitler's solution to Germany's problems is so simple," Daddy declared, "even an illiterate peasant can understand it: eliminate the Jews and you will eliminate your problems!"

"Is everyone taken in by such awful reasoning?" I asked.

"Of course not," Mama assured me. "In every place where Jews are threatened, there are some people of high moral principle who follow their conscience instead of their government, even at great risk to themselves."

"I believe Mr. Yeager was originally a German, judging from his accent," Daddy said. "Yet he is helping Jews."

The day wore on slowly, a torture of suspense and fear. Where would we go from here? We couldn't stay in a basement with no toilet, no kitchen, nowhere to sleep. At any moment, I thought, Mr. Yeager will return and move us to a more comfortable place. I was also afraid that at any moment I might hear Gestapo boots tramping down the stairs, invading our hiding place.

At dusk, Daddy put on his yarmulke, opened his prayerbook, and, facing East, began to recite the evening prayers. Where were the men, I wondered, who had worshiped with him only the night before. Mama took out the bread and cheese she had packed. Daddy finished his prayers and joined us on the flour sacks for our first dinner in hiding. We were careful not to eat too much. We had no idea how long our food would have to last.

When it was dark, Mama and Daddy arranged the flour sacks so that we could sleep near each other. During the night I thought I heard Mama crying softly.

"EEEEeeek, Mama," I heard myself scream later. Something—many things—were crawling all over me. I opened my eyes and in the weak morning light filtering into the basement I saw mice. They were everywhere: on the flour sacks, on my clothes, in my pockets, on my legs. I screamed again.

"Hush, hush," Mama whispered. "The mice will not hurt you, but the soldiers will if they hear your screams."

I jumped off my flour sack, frightening a score of mice into dark corners. Elie doubled over to keep himself from laughing aloud. But I didn't care if he laughed at me. I had been really scared.

That day passed much as the one before. The summer sun was strong, and as afternoon approached, the basement became very hot. No one came. Our feeling of isolation grew. To help pass the time Elie and I took turns looking out the window. Standing carefully to one side so that we couldn't be seen from outside, we had a clear view of Sommer Street down to the intersection at Leeuwerick

Street. There was very little happening on the deserted streets. Soldiers marched by occasionally, usually in pairs, their boots making a distinctive stomping sound on the cobblestones.

Late in the afternoon, I was looking through the window hoping to see a dog or cat, anything to relieve the tedium. Then I noticed a young boy walking on the other side of the street carrying a loaf of bread under one arm. I recognized him. He had been one of Elie's classmates. He was walking calmly in the direction of his house. I moved closer to the window.

"Halt!" someone shouted.

I hadn't noticed the soldier coming up the street in the opposite direction. The boy pretended not to hear the command and kept walking. That's right, I told him silently, act as though you don't realize he's talking to you.

"Halt!" the soldier barked again.

With what was clearly a great effort, the child kept walking steadily, passing the soldier on the other side of the street. I was sure he was following his parents' instructions not to run, no matter what. The soldier was talking to the child's back now.

"Halt!" he shouted a third time.

The boy never turned, never saw the soldier raise the rifle to his shoulder, never saw him take aim as casually as if he were shooting toy ducks in an amusement arcade. The shot rang out and the child fell. I gasped and stumbled away from the window.

"Why, Mama, why?" I sobbed into Mama's lap.

Too shaken to answer, she stroked my hair absentmindedly. When she looked at Daddy her eyes were full of meaning: see how right we were to hide; see what is happening to Jewish children whose lives were spared only yesterday!

I thought my family was not much different from the mice that had scurried away from me in fright that morning.

We were like small animals shivering in our hole, terrified of the more powerful animals outside. Were the soldiers afraid, too, I wondered, the way I had been afraid of the little mice?

While I sat on a flour sack wiping my eyes, I heard quiet footsteps on the stairs. Everyone turned. It was Mr. Yeager! We all sighed with relief and gathered around him to hear where the Resistance planned to send us.

8 · Hiding

July–December 1942

"Arrangements have been made for you to stay with a family named Adams," Mr. Yeager announced. "Clara, I think you know one of their sons. You will be taken to their home tonight, after dark. We must move you in two groups; you are less likely to arouse suspicion that way. Please make yourselves ready."

With a nod to Daddy and a quick bow to Mama he was gone as quickly and as quietly as he had come. We packed our few belongings. After Daddy said the evening prayers, we ate the last of our food and settled down once more to wait.

At nine o'clock, just as the sky was turning dark, Mr. Yeager returned with Mr. Adams. Adams was meek man, of average height, bald, and thin. He shook hands with Mama and Daddy. When they thanked him for helping us, he murmured that he was glad to do it. He was a trolley-car conductor and had obtained trolley tickets for everyone. Holding Elie's hand, Mama announced that she and Elie would go with Mr. Yeager. Daddy, Frieda, and I were to go with Mr. Adams.

The trip seemed endless, fraught with dangerous, unthinkable consequences. We were breaking so many regulations, traveling after curfew and sitting on the trolleys. But all this was necessary. We were pretending that we were not Jews, but Belgian citizens going about our normal business. Dear God, I prayed, please, please let us all arrive at Mr. Adams's house safely. Don't let any soldiers stop my family.

We arrived at a modest, two-story row house in a working-class neighborhood. As the two families were solemnly introduced to each other, the Adamses assured us that we were safe. They and their five children could be trusted not to tell anyone they were hiding Jews. Robert, the Adamses' oldest son, and I greeted each other gravely. We had been in some of the same classes in elementary school. Seeing a familiar face was somehow reassuring.

Mrs. Adams, a severe-looking woman, explained the living arrangements. Their family slept on the second floor. The first floor had four rooms. She led the way as we walked through the house. First was a living room, then a kitchen. Behind the kitchen was a small spare room. The only piece of furniture in the spare room was a narrow bed.

"This is your room," the woman announced. "The children will have to sleep on the floor."

We looked around our cramped quarters as she continued.

"You are to stay in your room except when you are preparing or eating your meals or using the bathroom. You will give me money to buy your food. Mrs. Heller, you may use the kitchen when I am out or when we are through eating. Under no circumstances are you to answer a knock on the door or look out a window. You will please remember that. Because we are hiding Jews, we are risking as much as you."

We nodded our understanding to each of her conditions. I sensed that she was not happy about our being in her house. Apparently, it had been Mr. Adams's idea to shelter Jews in danger. Mrs. Adams was cooperating only for the extra income we would provide.

At first it was strange to sleep on the floor in the same room as our parents and to spend whole days doing almost nothing, never going out. But we soon became accustomed to our surroundings, and our lives settled into a steady routine. Even though there were twelve people living in close quarters, sharing one bathroom and one kitchen, the two families lived completely independently of one another. Mrs. Adams had made it clear that this was the only way she could house another family. She and her husband were liberal-minded Catholics who felt that Jews were people like anyone else. But hiding them was strictly business.

On weekday mornings we stayed in our room until Mr. and Mrs. Adams were gone for the day. When school started in September, we heard the children getting ready to leave, Mrs. Adams preparing breakfast, Mr. Adams leaving for work. Once the house was quiet we were free to move about. Mrs. Adams spent most mornings at the local market. In the afternoon she liked to sit in the kitchen drinking whiskey, which made Mama nervous. We walked around the house without shoes and spoke in whispers, careful not to make any noise so that the neighbors on either side who shared walls with the Adamses would think the house was empty during the day. Each day was like the one before. There was no schedule. There was little to do. Our lives were punctuated by meals and by the coming and going of our hosts. We devised a system of knocks so that the Adamses could warn us if guests were coming. When we heard a warning knock, we all would run back to our room and wait in silence until the visitors left.

Of all the Adamses, Robert was the most sensitive to our situation. He often brought us games and books, and I thought he would have enjoyed spending more time with us had his mother not been so strict.

As days stretched into weeks, Mama and Daddy devised a program of instruction for us. They were worried about all the schooling we were missing, so part of every day was spent studying. Mama was fluent in many languages. We spoke Yiddish among ourselves; but when she was growing up in Romania, she had spoken Romanian and German as well. She had studied French in school and had learned Flemish and English in the ten years she had been in Belgium. She and Daddy knew Hungarian, too, which they spoke when they did not want us to understand what they were saying. Mama started to teach us all the languages she knew, with special emphasis on English.

Daddy discussed philosophy and history with us. He and Mama had always valued our opinions, so it seemed natural to us to examine our own situation with them in terms of history and ideas. Suddenly all the dry facts of Jewish history I had studied in school came alive as we talked. Daddy reminded us that the Jew's strength was also his burden. We had been persecuted through the ages because we had clung to our heritage. Our proud traditions and beliefs, which had become the basis for some of the world's other great religions, set us apart. We were fated always to appear different from other people, and this difference was often perceived by others as a threat. I had heard these words and ideas so many times—in classrooms, in synogogue, and in our home. But they never meant as much to me as when they were spoken in hiding, surrounded by terror and war. Daddy recounted the famous stories we all knew by heart: the Purim story about the struggle between Haman and the Jews of Shushan, when Esther's courage saved Jews from the gallows; the story of Masada, where Jews died rather than submit to Roman rule; the tales of the Spanish Inquisition, when the Marranos held fast to their Judaism in spite of the threat of torture and death by burning at the stake.

As my father spoke, a pattern began to emerge, a theme

that helped me to see our own situation as the latest event in the long struggle for freedom. I also understood the difference between our troubles and those of our ancestors. In the last hundred years the world had become industrialized, mechanized. Haman's power in a small city in Mesopotamia thousands of years before was greatly multiplied by Hitler, who had all the resources of a modern republic at his command. Hitler had the means to exterminate the entire Jewish population of Europe.

"Our job, our sacred duty," Daddy said, "is to stay alive. You must not see our hiding as an act of cowardice. We must survive in order to preserve Judaism. We are soldiers in the struggle for survival, and our battle is just as important as what is happening on the front."

When we were not having discussions or reading, we played games. Everyone took turns keeping Elie occupied, playing chess and checkers for hours. Sometimes, especially when I was reading a good book, I almost forgot where I was. But then my attention would drift, and I had the feeling that I was fading. Like words erased from a page, I seemed to exist only as a faint shadow.

Almost every afternoon when Mama went to the kitchen to prepare our evening meal, she found Mrs. Adams sitting at the kitchen table, a glass and a bottle of whiskey in front of her.

"A woman who drinks can't be trusted," Mama complained to Daddy. "How long will it be before she tells a neighbor about us?

"She's too frightened for her own safety to betray us," Daddy replied.

"She's using the money we pay her to buy liquor instead of food for her family," Frieda said.

"I don't think we can stay here much longer," insisted Mama. "And what about the Adams children? I'm so afraid that they'll let something slip, that they'll whisper their secret to a friend at school."

"They're terribly curious about us," I said. "Last

Sunday one of the little girls asked me why we don't go to church with them.''

Daddy tried to reassure us, saying that these were good people who had put themselves in a dangerous situation. But Mama could not stop worrying. I noticed that she was smoking more and more. She had always enjoyed cigarettes, but she had smoked only occasionally at home. Now it seemed that she was always holding a cigarette. She could no longer buy regular cigarettes, so we took turns rolling some tobacco in a little piece of paper. At first it was like a game, but soon she seemed to need cigarettes more than anything else.

Our most basic need in hiding was money. Without the money that we used to pay the Adamses, we could not imagine what would happen to us. They certainly could not afford to maintain us on their own, no matter how good their intentions. Our supply of money was shrinking, and our parents worried about it.

The day we went into hiding, Daddy had brought with him all the money he had in the house as well as a few diamonds. Now our cash was all gone, and Daddy had to sneak out at night every few weeks to meet a Christian friend who bought his gems. I was terribly frightened each time he went out and left us alone. I felt as though I hung suspended over a fearful chasm, dangling from a frayed rope. It was as if any sudden motion might destroy my precarious balance and I would plunge into a great nothingness. I knew that my behavior could not ensure Daddy's safety, but I needed to feel that by being very still I was helping him return to us unharmed.

The days wore on in tedious succession. Outside, Antwerp was dressing in fall colors. Children were scuffling through crisp leaves on the sidewalks. The parks and the zoo were less crowded now; the old people who lined the park benches in summer had gone inside. Children no longer sailed toy boats in the ponds, but there were lovers strolling through the park, oblivious to the weather. And there were young mothers pushing prams, their little ones swaddled in wools to protect them from the chilly air.

At the Adamses, fuel was in short supply. We had to put on extra sweaters. I began to spend long hours daydreaming about the world outside. I remembered the smell of burning leaves, the sight of giant elms, their golden leaves lit by the late afternoon sun, the sounds of children racing their bicycles in the park, laughing and shouting to one another. I longed for even a glimpse out the window.

"Just a little bit longer," Mama said when she saw me struggling against the confinement. "I'm sure it will be just a little bit longer."

Her calm certainty soothed my restlessness, and I went back to my book or played another game with Elie.

Our funds dwindled. We wondered whether the diamonds were still in their hiding place in the doorpost of our house on Leeuwerick Street. Elie wanted to go for the diamonds, but Mama and Daddy wouldn't let him. Such an errand would be terribly dangerous, they argued, and there was a good chance the diamonds were no longer there. We had heard rumors of empty Jewish homes being looted, both by Belgian citizens and by Nazi soldiers.

In December, just before Ḥanukkah, my parents decided that someone would have to go for the diamonds.

"I want to go," Elie insisted.

"He's too young. Let me go, Daddy," I begged.

"Perhaps it should be an adult," Mama said. "If you or I go, none of the children will be in danger."

"That's not fair," Elie cried. "I asked first."

We knew that it would probably be easier for a child to slip into the house unseen than a grownup, but Mama and Daddy hesitated exposing any of us to such danger. There seemed to be no way to settle the argument.

"Let's pick straws," I suggested. "The one who pulls the short straw runs the errand."

Mama and Daddy relented. We used five of Mama's matches. Daddy broke one off in the middle, then he held them between his thumb and forefinger with all the heads lined up evenly, the bottoms concealed in his fist. One by one we each picked a match. First Mama: she picked a long one. Then me. I pulled slowly, but it was long. Frieda pulled a long one also. There were two matches left. If Elie picked a long one, Daddy would go. Elie quickly pulled one match out of Daddy's hand. We all gasped; he had gotten his wish.

Daddy arranged for Mr. Adams to accompany Elie as close to Leeuwerick Street as possible. They would have to take several trolleys, and it would be dark. Elie would travel the last part of the journey on foot, alone. Mr. Adams agreed to wait for him at a designated spot.

They decided to go at nightfall. Everything had to be accomplished before the 7:00 P.M. curfew. Anyone on the street after that hour could be questioned, even shot by patrolling soldiers.

The streets were busy with people going home from work. Mama bundled Elie up warmly in coats and scarves borrowed from the Adams children, holding him close for a few moments as though she wished her love could protect him. When Elie and Mr. Adams were both ready, Mama gave Elie one last embrace, Daddy shook their hands, we all whispered, "Good luck," and then they were out the door, swallowed by the night. I envied Elie his errand, not only because he was doing something important, but because he was outside, breathing fresh air.

We sat in our room and waited. We had spent months waiting, but this was a special kind of torment. Mama started smoking nervously, one cigarette after another. Her broad, handsome face, usually so calm, was contorted with worry. Daddy sat on the edge of the bed, his elbows on his knees, holding his head in his hands.

In our minds we were all with Elie. I could picture every part of his trip. I imagined him sitting on the trolley. There would be soldiers everywhere. Elie had been instructed to behave calmly. Thank goodness it's so cold, I thought, with that hat on, no one can see how dark and curly his hair is. If a soldier questioned him, Elie would reply in Flemish. Once Elie and Mr. Adams were across town they would have to travel on foot. This was as dangerous as riding the trolley because our entire neighborhood had been emptied that night in July. Anyone entering an uninhabited street after dark would look suspicious to a soldier on patrol. Alone and without lights, Elie had to go to our house, remove the doorframe, retrieve the packet, and return to where Mr. Adams waited for him.

One hour passed, and another. I could not even think about the possibility that Elie might get caught or that he might not get the diamonds. The hour for curfew was approaching. Just when I felt I would explode from tension, we heard the front door open. We stayed in our room in case it was guests for the Adams family—or worse. Then we heard running footsteps, and Elie burst into the room. He tumbled into Frieda's arms and said, "I got them! I got them!" He laughed hysterically and yelled, "I got them! I got the *lokshen*! I got them!"

After so much hardship, Elie's success made us all deliriously happy. We suddenly took delight in the code word we used for diamonds—*lokshen* (noodles)—and laughed with him. "He's got them. He's got the *lokshen*," we laughed, so hard that we were soon panting and once again mindful that we had to keep quiet.

That night, despite our confinement, our joy was complete. Elie's triumph belonged to all of us. He told us that he had found the house in a shambles. People had stripped it bare of furniture and had searched everywhere but the secret doorframe for hidden treasure. Floor boards were torn up, wallpaper was ripped from the wall, even the stairs had been destroyed.

A week later, on the last night in December, Daddy went out to sell one of the stones Elie had retrieved.

9 · Wandering

December 30, 1942

When Daddy didn't return that night, Mama refused to let us worry. As it got later and later, she reasoned that his business had lasted beyond curfew and he was probably staying at his friend's house overnight. Even the next morning, when he still hadn't returned, Mama felt that there would be a logical explanation. None of us was prepared for the shock that awaited us.

A policeman whom we knew from our neighborhood, a member of the Resistance, stood at the door to our room later that morning, nervously twisting his hat in his hands.

"Good morning, Mrs. Heller," he stammered. "I wish I didn't have to bring you such terrible news."

I instinctively moved to Mama's side.

"I was at the station early this morning when a man came in to report a suicide. He told us that Sholom Heller had gassed himself in his apartment the night before."

I didn't understand what the officer was saying. Was he

really talking about my father? There must be a mistake. Daddy only went out to get some money. Then I heard Mama's cry, and I knew it was all true.

"Gassed himself?" Mama cried, "It's a lie! He's thirty-seven years old. He has everything to live for! He was killed for whatever he had in his pockets. Sholom would never commit suicide; he's a religious Jew!"

After this outburst she sat down heavily on the bed, her head in her hands. We looked first at the policeman, then at Mama as the awful reality sank in.

After a few minutes, Mama composed herself and made arrangements for Daddy's burial. She took his tallith from among his belongings and handed it to the officer.

"Please see to it that my husband is wrapped in this," she said, speaking with great effort.

The policeman explained that there could be no real funeral, nor would Daddy be buried in a Jewish cemetery because of Nazi regulations. However, he would see that Daddy was wrapped in the tallith and he promised that the truck bearing Daddy's coffin would pass our hiding place the next morning on its way to the cemetery.

Mama sat on the edge of the bed in stony silence for the rest of the day. I cried quietly, hardly able to believe that my beloved father was really gone. The next morning we stood by the window and peeked through a slit in the closed curtains. At about ten o'clock Daddy's pitiful funeral cortege passed in front of us. First, driving a patrol car, came the policeman who had told us about Daddy. Behind him was an open truck carrying the coffin.

When the truck was out of sight, Mama stumbled back to our room and collapsed on the bed. She lay there day after day, unaware of anything happening around her, without speaking, eating, or even smoking. Once in a while we managed to have her drink a little broth. I thought that she, too, might die. Mr. Adams contacted a doctor who worked with the Resistance. The doctor explained that she had suffered an emotional collapse. We must keep her alive by encouraging her to eat and drink. When the shock of Daddy's death had passed, he assured us, she would recover.

I was frightened. I had never been so alone. We had always relied on Daddy and Mama. But now all that had changed. With Daddy gone and Mama lying helpless, it suddenly occurred to me that Elie, Frieda, and I were on our own.

Why was this happening? What was my crime, and how could God let something like this happen? I had not prayed since Belgium had fallen to the Nazis, but now I felt torn inside. Part of me wanted to pray, but part of me questioned my faith in God.

I sat and waited. And thought. At first I thought about how my life had been destroyed and about how God had let that happen. Then I felt a great anger at Daddy's friend. Daddy had known him for over ten years. How could he have done this? What kind of beast would kill a friend just to steal his diamonds? I clenched my fists and hoped I would someday be able to beat him with my own hands. I felt hungry for air and longed for it and dreamed of the day I would once again be able to breathe, free and in the open.

For one long week Mama lay in bed. I had almost lost hope when, late in the afternoon of the seventh day, she sat up slowly and said, "Clara, please roll a cigarette for me."

I leaped for the packet of cigarette papers and the tobacco pouch that had lain unused by her bed all week. My hands trembled as I rolled a cigarette. If Mama wanted to smoke again, she must be getting well. She would be back in charge.

While she was recuperating, Mama became convinced that we had stayed at the Adamses long enough. It was only a matter of time, she was certain, before someone told the authorities we were there. When a man from the Resistance came to check on us, as he did every week, Mama discussed her worries with him.

"I agree, Mrs. Heller," he said. "The Gestapo has started making systematic searches in different neighborhoods. From now on no location will be safe for long. We'll keep in touch. We'll tell you when it's time to move."

During the next few months, the winter of 1943, we lived in a bewildering succession of places, sometimes alone, sometimes with other people. Occasionally, the Resistance would leave small children with us for a few days while they found Christian families willing to hide them. One member of the Resistance, a petite, attractive woman named Blanchka, became very close to Mama, and we looked forward to her visits. She and Mama sat and talked, and the worry lines on Mama's face turned into smiles. We learned that Blanchka was helping many Jews in hiding, and, through Blanchka, Mama learned of others she knew who had survived the roundups.

When we left the Adamses' house, we were first hidden in the attic of an old house on Beems Street overlooking the Scheldt River. Before the war, my friends and I loved to walk along the waterfront in this area of town, watching the activities of the big, busy port. Now I could only imagine what was happening outside, for the windows of our attic had been painted white. No one could see into our hiding place. And we couldn't see out.

Below us was a nightclub where Nazi soldiers came during the evening to drink and be entertained. During the day, when the house was still, we slept or read, washed clothes, and played quiet games. At nightfall, men began arriving downstairs, and we heard music and laughter and soldiers' boots on the stairs. We sat in the dark, listening, afraid to light even a candle for fear it would be noticed by one of the visitors. If the whole situation weren't so dangerous, I thought, it would be funny. There we were, not ten meters away from the German army, and they had no idea that Jews were sitting right above their heads!

When Blanchka learned that the Gestapo was conducting raids in the houses along the Scheldt, she moved us to a three-story house on Helene Lane. A group of men, some in their late teens and early twenties, and others much older, had been hiding there for some months. I was fascinated by the stories the young men told. Several had escaped from detention camps. They spent long afternoons sitting at the kitchen table recounting the horrors they had seen. None of them knew my brother Heshie. I wondered if we would ever hear from him again.

When the young men told how Jews were loaded into airless vans on hot summer days, how hundreds were crowded into railroad cars to be shipped eastward, some of the older men accused them of lying.

"Why would we make up such stories?" the young men asked.

"You want to get us all killed," was the reply. "You think that if we get angry enough, we'll try to fight the Nazis. Just sit quietly. Soon the whole business will be over."

After we left the attic on Beems Street, Frieda started going out again. She ran small errands for Mama and sometimes found a child or an elderly Jew wandering in the street and brought him to us for protection. Her activities frightened us, but Mama felt that she needed some freedom in order to endure hiding. In spite of the danger, Frieda loved the adventure of going out. She was always full of information when she came back. It was Frieda who warned Mama that there might be informers in the house, people who would betray us to the Nazis in return for money or favors. She had heard rumors that, because of these collaborators, our house would probably be raided soon.

"Clara," Mama said as soon as she heard this news, "you must warn Blanchka. We have to leave."

That night I sneaked out of the house and walked many blocks to Blanchka's.

"There are collaborators at Helene Lane," I blurted as soon as she opened the door. "Mama says we have to leave."

"Oh, my God," Blanchka said, instantly believing my report. "I hope it's not too late. Give me a few hours. I'll do what I can."

But my errand had come too late. Later that evening, after I had returned from Blanchka's, there was a strange knock on the front door. No one answered it. It was not our secret code. The knock came again. In our room, the four of us looked at each other, immobilized by terror.

We heard harsh orders shouted from outside. "Open up in the name of the Third Reich, or we will shoot everyone in there."

"Quick," Mama whispered, "Clara, help me get this window open."

I couldn't move. People were in the hall now, crying in desperation. It was like the night they had rounded up everyone who lived on our street. I was reliving a familiar nightmare. I was too frightened to move and unable to cry for help.

"Clara!" Mama's whispered command jolted me out of my trance. Together we opened the window.

"Elie, you go first," Mama whispered.

I looked around to see Elie pressed against the wall across from the window, next to the door.

"I'll go last," he said. "You all go ahead of me."

Elie was tired of hiding. He often talked about giving up. They were going to get us anyway, he insisted. Why prolong the game? Elie saw the look in my eyes that said I knew what he was planning.

"Don't be silly, Clara. I'm coming. You go first."

With every muscle quivering, I climbed onto the windowsill and thrust my feet over the edge. Turning over onto my stomach, I lowered my body as far as I could, my hands clutching the sill.

"Please, God, don't let anyone see me," I prayed silently, my eyes clenched shut. Then I jumped. The ground was soft and damp from the spring rains, cushioning my fall and soaking my stocking feet. Frieda landed beside me. Instinctively, we flattened ourselves against the wall, wishing we could melt into it.

"Catch!" Mama whispered down to us. She had managed to throw some of our clothes and belongings into a bag which now landed in my outstretched hands. In a moment Mama, too, was standing beside us. Elie scrambled over the window ledge, landing next to me.

The shouting at the front door had become louder. Now we heard boots and rifle butts striking the door to force it open.

"Come," Mama whispered, "we can't stay here."

We ran through the backyard and into an alley behind the row of houses on Helene Lane. When we stopped for breath, Mama spotted a door in a garden wall. Opening it cautiously, she motioned for us to enter. Once inside, we huddled against the fence at the farthest corner, shivering from fear and the damp night.

"Children, you must stay right here while I go for help," Mama said in a hushed voice. "I'll be back as soon as I can. Just stay still."

"Let us go with you," I begged.

"No," she insisted. "You'll be fine here for a few minutes. I'll be right back."

Wet and cold, we crouched against the wall. Mama returned about an hour later. She had found Blanchka at home. Again, Blanchka promised to do everything she could "Give me a few hours," she had told Mama. We clung to each other and waited.

It was Kroll, a worker for the Resistance, who found us. We were wet and shivering, huddled against the fence. As we walked through the back streets of Antwerp, he helped us piece together the events that had taken place since I contacted Blanchka that afternoon. Mama's instincts had been right. The Gestapo raid had been planned for some time, but the Resistance found out about it too late. Kroll received Blanchka's urgent message and, earlier in the evening, went to Helene Lane to get us. Standing in the shadows half a block away, he watched as more than a dozen people were pushed and shoved out of the house and onto waiting army trucks. He assumed that we had been captured. Later, when he reported to his Resistance leader, he learned that we were alive and waiting for him. He led us to a barroom in a run-down section of the city. This was to be our emergency quarters until he and Blanchka could find another place for us to live. The room was cluttered with chairs and tables and smelled of beer.

"This is the best we can do for now," he said. "Make yourselves comfortable. I'll see you in the morning."

We hung our wet stockings on the bar to dry, and curled up on tables to sleep. It was very dark and we felt safe, but sleep would not come. Quietly, we whispered for hours about what had happened.

We lived at the tavern for three days, sleeping in the barroom at night, hiding in a cramped storeroom during the day. From there we were transferred to a house that had recently been raided by the Gestapo, its residents carried away. Kroll and Blanchka reasoned that we would be safe there for a short time because the Nazis had emptied it so recently. We were alone, but the tension was almost unbearable. How long would it take the Nazis to discover that the house was occupied once more by Jews? Our next lodging was a storeroom in a telephone office building. There was a toilet at the end of the hall, but we could only use it at night when the building was empty. Blanchka had to bring us our meals. For several weeks, she was the only other person we saw.

I never got used to living with fear. I didn't sleep. I listened to every creak, every street noise for hints, warning sounds that doom had arrived and the long struggle to live, to outwit the enemy was over. I understood Elie's longing to be done with the struggle. But what would happen to us if we let ourselves be caught? No one could be sure what lay beyond the army trucks and railroad cars. Some of the stories we had heard seemed too horrible to be true. Perhaps they were just anti-Nazi propaganda. And yet not to believe them seemed more rash than our efforts to hide. The people who worked with the Resistance were convinced that Jews who were taken away had no chance at all. We had no choice. We had to keep hiding, running, living with fear.

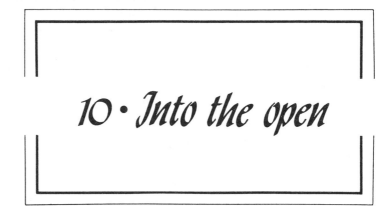

10 · Into the open

March 1943

Spring came to Antwerp unseen by our little family group. I imagined the pale green leaves that must have been sprouting from the poplar and linden trees. In the countryside I knew the farmers were plowing their fields, and children and dogs were racing up and down beside the canals. We had missed almost a year and a half of school. What would I become, I wondered, without a proper education? Mama was more worried about our teeth and bones.

"You will have time to learn," she liked to remind us, "but you won't have another chance to grow."

We hardly ever ate fresh fruits, vegetables, or meat. I didn't tell Mama, but I was thankful that our meals consisted mainly of bread and boiled potatoes, with an occasional piece of fish or a head of cabbage. My teeth hurt if I bit into anything hard.

We were not Belgian citizens. Our identification papers, which proved that we were Romanian citizens, had saved us from being rounded up that first night almost a year before. We had gone into hiding not because we were Romanians, but because we were Jews. Then, in the late spring of 1943, there were notices in the newspapers telling Romanian citizens that it was safe for them to live in the open, that they would not be bothered by the Gestapo, whether they were Jewish or not. Romanian Jews were expected to go back to their homes.

We desperately wanted to leave our hiding place, to live normally again. Mama, Kroll, and Blanchka talked about the new situation for several days. Kroll and Blanchka watched to see if the Nazis would keep their word or if they were baiting a trap to lure all the Romanian Jews out of hiding. Mama flatly refused to go back to our house on Leeuwerick Street. Our old neighborhood was empty. There we would be conspicuous, vulnerable to any new Nazi whim. Our two saviors agreed that it would be foolish to take such a chance. Instead, they felt we would be safe living quietly in the open among sympathetic neighbors.

A priest from the Resistance, a friend of Kroll's, found a small house for us in a poor Catholic neighborhood. The house was flanked by two larger residences, one for priests, the other for nuns. Inside, it was dark and almost bare. The front door opened on a narrow living room. A scratchy horsehair sofa stood against one wall, with two straight wooden chairs opposite it. Behind the living room was a small kitchen. There were a few dishes, two pots, and a meager supply of eating utensils. The kitchen was dominated by a square wooden table covered with an old oilcloth. A bare bulb hung from the ceiling and swayed eerily on windy evenings. Whoever had lived there must have been very poor.

In spite of the bareness of the house, we were happy to be living on our own. We enjoyed sitting near the windows and looking outside, cooking our own meals and running cautious little errands. We lived openly but carefully, waiting for the Nazis to be conquered, for the war to be over.

Mama never felt that we were really safe, so there was no thought of running and playing outdoors. There were soldiers everywhere. We spent most of the time inside the house waiting, as we had for the past year. There were days when I never bothered to get dressed. For us children it was a time filled with both tension and boredom. I am alive, I thought, but that is all.

For Mama, however, the move to the Nuns' and Priests' house, as we called it, brought with it a surge of contacts with the outside world. Our Catholic neighbors took a special protective interest in us, seeing that we never lacked for food or clothing and, more important, providing a source of constant companionship for Mama.

Nearly every afternoon one or two sisters stopped in to say hello. In the evenings the priests, several of whom Mama had known before the war, sat at our kitchen table talking for hours over "ersatz"—that is, artificial—wartime coffee. These conversations were political and philosophical, and it was wonderful to see my mother's face light up during a stimulating discussion.

One of the priests, Father Buchhalter, was really a Jew in disguise. He worked with the Resistance, hiding his identity behind the black suit and white collar of the clergy. Mother had known him only slightly before the war, but now he became our special friend, dropping by every few days, surprising us with little packages of food. Mama confided to him her anxiety about what had happened to our house on Leeuwerick Street. We had learned nothing more since Elie's visit the previous December to retrieve the diamonds.

Buchhalter went to visit the house and confirmed Elie's report. It had been completely ransacked, he said, the flooring and stairs torn up, the wallpaper ripped off the walls. Every piece of furniture had been removed. The soda factory was ankle deep in broken glass. Someone had systematically smashed hundreds of glass bottles to remove the lead tops, which could be melted down for ammunition.

Now we knew. All our thoughts about resuming, even

partially, the life we had left disappeared. I felt as though my memories had been smashed like our furniture. My identity had been scattered about like so much broken glass. I realized for the first time that if we lived through our present trials, we would have to build a new life, piece by piece, a life that would have little in common with the one we had lost.

While we were living with the nuns and priests, our passports expired. At first, Mama couldn't decide what to do. Our passports proved our Romanian citizenship. They had to be renewed in Brussels, the capital of Belgium, which was about forty-five minutes away by train. Should she risk the trip, she wondered. What would happen after the authorities realized we were still alive? On the other hand, things might be worse for us if we were caught without up-to-date papers. Our Romanian citizenship had protected us thus far. It seemed foolish to be without it.

Except for our occasional errands, Elie, Frieda, and I had not spent any time without Mama in the months since Daddy had died. We dreaded her making the long trip to Brussels and back alone, but she insisted that we stay behind. She would not risk our lives as well as her own.

"And furthermore," she assured us as she was preparing to leave, "all our papers are in order. I won't have any trouble with the authorities. You'll see, I'll be back by dinner."

As she went out the door she called back, "I wrote out the words of an old song for you. It's on the kitchen table. Frieda knows the tune. I'd like to hear you sing it to me when I come home."

I began to cry at the beauty of her gesture, the thought she had given to how we were to spend the long day waiting for her return. Of course, we needed something to work on, to accomplish by the time she got home. In the old days it would have been a book or a new game which she had saved to give us as she went out with Daddy for the evening. How sad and how beautiful, I thought, that she is still giving us gifts. I ran to find the paper. Frieda's lilting soprano filled the room with the haunting Yiddish melody. I hummed in the background, trying to learn the words.

Zol zein az ich boi in der luft meiner shlesser;
Zol zein az di shif vet nit komen zum brek;
In troim iz mir shenner, in troim iz mir besser,
In cholem der himmel iz bloier vi bloi.

It may be that I build my castles in the air;
It may be that my ship will never come in;
But my dreams are so beautiful, my dreams are so good,
The skies in my dream are bluer than blue.

When it was dinner time we started looking out the window every few minutes, hoping to catch the first glimpse of Mama as she came down the street. Soon it began to get dark. We started pacing nervously, our tempers shortened by the long hours of waiting.

"We should have gone, too," Frieda insisted. "Then we'd be together no matter what happens."

"But you know what Mama always tells us, Frieda," I said sharply. "We don't take risks that could put us all in danger. Someone must survive."

We all jumped as we heard knocking on the door. It came again. Still, we didn't answer. Then we heard the familiar voice of the druggist who owned the pharmacy.

"It's all right, children. It's me, Mr. Vandenrein. I have a message from your mother."

Frieda opened the door cautiously.

"Don't look so frightened, children," he said, smiling. "Your mother is all right. Her business in Brussels took longer than she expected. She phoned me so that I could let you know not to worry."

We thanked Mr. Vandenrein again and again. After he

left, we hugged each other for joy and started to prepare dinner.

Later, I would be grateful for the casual way in which Mr. Vandenrein told us Mama would be home soon. He knew that she was having trouble renewing our passports, but he was careful not to let us know his concern. When Mama finally arrived, exhausted but relieved to be back, I cried, realizing how very alone I had felt without her.

"Stop this crying, Clara," she said, smiling through her own tears. "Give me something to eat, and I'll tell you all about my day."

The train had been crowded that morning, filled with business people, workers, and soldiers traveling south. There were a lot of army personnel, but none making an official search of the passengers' papers. Only the ticket collector had talked to Mama during the entire journey. Once in Brussels, she took a trolley to the Staat House, the City Hall, again without incident. She was not wearing the yellow star, feeling that it would attract attention. Yet if her papers were examined, she realized, she might be arrested for traveling without it. Either way was risky.

At the Staat House she went first to the office of the Romanian ambassador. She was hoping that she could have the papers restamped there and avoid dealing with the German authorities. But at the ambassador's office they told her that, because the family had been living outside Romania for more than ten years, that office could no longer process our passports. The Gestapo would have to approve everything.

It took several hours of standing in different lines to get all the required signatures and stamps. Mama saw a Jewish man whom she knew standing in another line. She was certain he recognized her as well, but they pretended not to know one another. The officials asked questions about our whereabouts, and that made her anxious. When the last of the documents was stamped and Mama started to leave, the

Nazi official behind the desk asked her to please wait until the commandant had approved everything.

Mama thought her heart would stop.

"But there's nothing for him to approve," she protested politely. "Everything is in order. You told me so yourself."

"I understand, Madam, but that is the policy. You may not leave until you have seen him."

All at once Mama felt as helpless as she had felt when Daddy died. She sat on a wooden bench in the waiting room thinking that all our efforts to survive could be destroyed with one stroke of the commandant's pen. She waited one hour, then another. Soon it was past the time when she had promised to be home. There were still several people ahead of her. Taking a chance, she told the secretary she had to go to the ladies' room, but once outside the waiting room she dashed outdoors and ran to a pay phone. She spoke quickly to Mr. Vandenrein and asked him to do two things: first, he was to tell us that she was all right; second, more importantly, she begged him to make certain that we were safe.

Finally, she was brought before the commandant.

"State your name, Frau," he ordered.

Mama replied. The officer's voice went on and on, asking one question after another. Mama answered, trying to concentrate on what was required of her, wondering fearfully whether he would notice that she wasn't wearing the yellow star, whether we were safe at home, whether she had said anything to compromise our situation, whether they had kept her waiting while soldiers were sent to arrest us. She now understood, she told us, what it meant to be interrogated. She realized what other Jews were enduring. She was aware, also, that the officer was enjoying her discomfort. Whereas she was in a desperate hurry to return to Antwerp, he had nothing to do but to satisfy himself that this attractive Jewish woman was complying with all the rules and regulations imposed by the Nazi occupation.

At long last, having satisfied himself that there were no

loopholes in her papers through which German law could reach to round up what remained of the Heller family, he reluctantly let her go. Clutching the documents, Mama concentrated on making herself as inconspicuous as possible on the long ride home.

We had hoped to wait out the war in the safety and comfort of the little house between the nuns and the priests. However, Mama's journey to Brussels had shaken her confidence. Reluctantly, she began talking to Kroll and Blanchka about moving once more. But the decision to go back into hiding was painful to make, and Mama put it off. Then an extraordinary incident helped us come to a decision.

Early one morning, Mama was sitting by the window in the living room reading after a sleepless night. Two Belgian women walking to market stopped to chat directly below her window.

"Did you hear," one of them said, "they rounded up all the Belgian Jews last night?"

"Is that right?" asked the other.

"Yes. Gestapo knocked on all the doors of families whose addresses they knew."

The women walked on, still chatting, leaving Mama trying to gather her thoughts and make sense out of what she had just heard. The women may have been trying to give her a message without endangering themselves. In any case, Mama knew what to do.

"Hurry, hurry," she urged as a minute later she roused us roughly out of our sleep. "We have to run again."

Drowsily, we threw our belongings into our small bags and walked to a safe house that Frieda knew the Resistance used in emergencies. There we found Resistance workers who contacted others for us. They confirmed what Mama had overheard. It was true. The night before, the Gestapo had rounded up the remaining Jews who, like us, had believed Nazi assurances that they could now live in the open. The mistake Jews were making over and over was believing that the Nazis acted out of regard for order or reason. In truth, their tactics were aimed at creating confusion, indecision, insecurity, and general chaos in the Jewish community. It was as though we were taking part in a huge game of death. If a player could survive long enough, he might eventually figure out the rules. Unfortunately, few players remained after one or two rounds.

From the safe house, where we could only stay for a few hours, Kroll took us to a farm outside the city limits. There we hid in a hayloft while he searched for a hiding place. Twice a day the farmer brought us food and asked if we were all right. On the evening of the third day the farmer returned to move us to our new accommodations. We had to go separately, first Frieda and Elie, then Mama and me, because a crowded car was more likely to be stopped by a suspicious soldier than one holding only two or three people. I was happy to be leaving the barn, yet I wondered what dreadful place the farmer was taking us to now.

11 · Mrs. Brussels

April 1943

We drove in silence toward Antwerp. I crouched low in the back seat, afraid of being spotted by a soldier on patrol, yet enjoying the motion of the car and the momentary feeling of freedom. As we approached the darkened city, I stole glances at the passing streets. The windows of the buildings were hung with blackout curtains, looking as though they had closed their eyes on the Jews, shutting out the sight of our pain and our wanderings.

The car passed through the outskirts of town and made its way toward a fashionable section. Our progress was slow because the tops of our headlights were painted over with dark paint to prevent their being seen from the air. We stopped in front of one of the stately old mansions on Frankrichlei—the French Boulevard. I looked in amazement. We had never hidden in such a nice house.

"Last stop," the farmer said gently, trying to put us at ease.

He led us around to the back of the house. We might have attracted attention going up the front steps in our stocking feet, our clothes prickly with bits of hay from the barn. Once inside, he led us through a big kitchen and up two flights of stairs. I caught glimpses of rich draperies, delicate china figurines, and a grand piano in the living room as I passed by. Frieda and Elie were waiting for us on the third floor with Mrs. Brussels, our new host.

The farmer introduced us. She was tall and fair-haired, dressed in stylish, well-cut clothes. Her manner was welcoming but distant, as though she did not want to grow fond of anyone whose life was in danger and who, as of that moment, would endanger her own. After the farmer left, Mrs. Brussels told us that her husband was Jewish. He had been taken away by the Gestapo early in the war. In her anger and frustration, she had begun to cooperate with the Resistance. It made her feel better to think that she was helping fight the people who had caused her so much suffering. She showed us the three rooms that made up the third floor, and said that we would be free to move about the house as long as we stayed away from the windows and doors.

Hiding at Mrs. Brussels's house was more pleasant than anywhere else we had been. Our quarters were large, filled with light during the day, warm and comfortable at night. Mama had her own room, a luxury she had not expected to enjoy so soon again. Frieda, Elie, and I shared another room. The front bedroom served as our sitting room. There was a library on the first floor, its shelves lined with beautiful editions of books on all subjects. Elie and I read volumes by the great Russian writers Tolstoy and Dostoyevsky. Dostoyevsky was my favorite. His stories helped me forget the slow hours. Elie read everything he could—history, philosophy, literature. When he discussed books with us, it was hard to remember how young he was. Frieda loved to play the piano, which she was allowed to do when Mrs. Brussels was at home. That way, if one of the neighbors noticed the music, Mrs. Brussels could say she was playing.

Late one afternoon Frieda was in the living room playing the piano. Mrs. Brussels was in the back of the house. Elie, Mama, and I were upstairs reading and taking turns listening to the tiny radio Mrs. Brussels had given us. We could hear strains of Frieda's favorite arias drifting up the stairs. Danger seemed very far away in that elegant house. We were all convinced that the war could not last much longer, and we felt fortunate to be so comfortable and so safe.

Sitting at the piano, her back to the hall, Frieda heard a key turn in the front door lock. She froze, confused, not knowing whether to dash for the stairs or run to the back of the house. Before she could move, the door opened and a young man and woman burst in, breathless, their faces flushed from running. Frieda stared at them. The young woman was older than Frieda. She was tall, her long blonde hair rolled into a fashionable bun at the nape of her neck. Her companion was even taller, with fair hair and steel-rimmed glasses.

"Who are you?" the woman asked Frieda, clearly surprised to see a stranger at the piano.

"I'm a friend of Mrs. Brussels," Frieda replied hesitantly. "She lets me come here sometimes to play her piano."

"Oh, hello, then," the young woman said, "I'm Billie, and this is my friend Klaas. Mrs. Brussels is my mother."

At that moment, to Frieda's relief, Mrs. Brussels, having heard their voices, came in from the kitchen. There were greetings all around. Billie, she explained to Frieda, was living with friends while she attended school. Frieda stayed seated at the piano, hoping the visitors would not notice that she wasn't wearing shoes. Mrs. Brussels confirmed Frieda's story that she was a neighbor, and they chatted for what seemed to Frieda an eternity about the war and school. When the door finally closed behind them, Mrs.

Brussels heaved a sigh of relief and told Frieda not to worry, their secret was still safe.

"We will just have to be more careful about your piano playing," she said. "Don't worry about other people. Billie is the only one who has a key to the house."

Mama, too, made light of the incident.

"What if the young man had been in uniform?" she teased Frieda. "Then you really would have had a problem."

But we all knew it was no laughing matter. From then on we were more cautious.

Nature takes no notice of man, and, as spring came to an embattled Europe, Mrs. Brussels's house was filled with lilac blooms whose fragrance aroused memories within me of happier springs. Each night we listened to the BBC broadcasts, which now spoke of significant Allied victories. As Passover approached, we felt confident that we would celebrate next year's seder in freedom.

We couldn't have a real seder. We had no Haggadah to read the service from, and it was impossible to buy matzo, the traditional unleavened bread. But Mama made our simple meal as festive as possible, and we talked about the Passover story. I felt a special kinship with those Jews of long ago who had fled from slavery into freedom. When we closed our little service with the traditional "Next year in Jerusalem," I understood that ancient wish in a new light and wondered if there would ever be a place that Jews could call home.

After dinner, upstairs in our sitting room, we listened to the BBC. The reception on our radio was so faint that we took turns pressing our ears against the speaker and repeating the news to each other. Mama fiddled with the dial until she heard the four opening notes of Beethoven's Fifth Symphony that announced a BBC broadcast. She listened for a few minutes, then suddenly switched the radio off. I glanced up and saw a look of startled horror on her face.

"It's unbelievable," she gasped.

"What is it, Mama?" Elie asked.

"Warsaw. The Jews are fighting in the ghetto."

Yes, I thought, the Nazis always attack us on Jewish holidays. It had been that way throughout the war. Our neighborhood was cleared out on the Sabbath. Kroll and Blanchka had told us that that was the usual Nazi practice.

"Turn the radio on, Mama," Frieda begged.

"You listen," she replied. "Tell me what's going on. I can't bear to hear it."

Each of us took turns listening. We heard that the Nazis were meeting armed resistance in the Warsaw ghetto. We knew that many thousands of Jews had been forced to live in a walled-off area. We had heard rumors of overcrowding and food shortages. Then we had heard that there were roundups, like those we had witnessed in Antwerp. But how had the Jews obtained weapons? And how did they have the courage to oppose an entire army?

For four weeks, from April 19 to May 16, 1943, we listened to reports of the battle. At first, Mama was afraid that we, too, would want to fight the Nazis. But as the days wore on, we realized with sickening certainty that the ghetto uprising was doomed. We could only imagine what suffering was being endured by the handful of Jews left amid the ashes. Yet the uprising was a source of pride for us.

"Look at what Jews are doing," Frieda said again and again. "They are showing the world that we can fight, that we have courage and strength. They are humiliating the entire German army."

How can the world stand by and watch this happen, I thought. But by then I knew there was no answer to my question.

When we heard that the Nazis had burned the ghetto in order to liquidate the remaining Jews, we mourned the inevitable tragedy. But we remained proud of the struggle.

One morning in June, Mrs. Brussels told us she had a bad toothache. She was waiting for a call from the dentist to let her know when she could be seen. One look at her told me she was in pain. Her normally neat hair was mussed, and her face showed the strain of having been awake all night. She had fastened a towel like a sling around her head and under her chin to ease the pressure in her jaw. She hoped the call would come soon, and we agreed to stay on the third floor so that the house would seem empty when she left.

It was one of those sultry June days that announces summer's arrival. Hardly a leaf stirred outside, and all our windows were open to encourage the smallest breeze to fan the warm rooms. Mama, Frieda, Elie, and I were reading in our sitting room when, amid the normal street noises, we heard a truck come to a stop in front of the house. Doors opened and shut, and there was the sound of heavy footsteps on the front stairs. Mama peeked through the lace curtains at the window overlooking the street.

"My God," she whispered, "They're coming."

Her words sent a shiver of fear through me. She straightened herself, and with a hard, determined look said, "Let's go with dignity."

I ran to hide in a closet. I won't make it easy for them to find me, I thought. But if they find the others, I'll go with them. Crouching in the closet, I left the door open a crack to hear what was happening.

There was a sharp knock on the door, then Mrs. Brussels's footsteps, not hurrying, as she went to answer it.

"You are hiding *Juden*," I heard a male voice announce.

"No," came Mrs. Brussels's reply in a strong voice.

"We know there are Jews here."

There was a clatter of feet. They must have pushed Mrs. Brussels out of the doorway because I heard her say, "I'm a sick woman. Can't you see I'm sick? You have no right to force your way in here like this."

"Search the house," the man's voice ordered.

"Go ahead, look all you like," Mrs. Brussels dared them. "There's no one here but me."

"Be careful," she shouted a moment later. "Those figurines are valuable. What do you think you're doing? I am a Belgian citizen. What makes you think I have strangers in my house?"

She kept up a steady chatter of loud complaining as the men made their way from room to room, opening and slamming doors and moving furniture. Then there was the sound of boots mounting the stairs to the second floor. More opening and closing of doors and then, impatiently, "There's no one here sir."

"All right, let's get going."

Unbelievably, incredibly, they had not searched the third floor. Now the boots were descending the stairs, and I heard the front door shut. And then silence. I listened to the truck start up and drive away. After a minute or two I unfolded myself from the closet and walked out, half expecting a trap, a soldier in the sitting room waiting to grab me. But there were Mama and Frieda and Elie sitting as I had left them. It was a while before anyone spoke.

"We'll have to go somewhere else," Mama whispered at last. "Frieda, tonight you'll contact Kroll."

Frieda nodded.

Mrs. Brussels did not come upstairs to see us the rest of that day. We heard her leave for the dentist and return. There was nothing to discuss. It was too dangerous for her to hide us any longer. We had thought we could wait out the war in the comfort and security of the big house on Frankrichlei. The end had seemed so close. We gathered our few belongings together and waited to be taken to yet another place.

12 · Anneke

1944

For the next three months we moved constantly, but we never lived anywhere as pleasant as Mrs. Brussels's. Blanchka and Kroll brought us food, buoyed our spirits with the latest news, and tried to assure us that we would survive. We were fortunate to have each other. In most of the places we were hidden, there were only adults. Many parents had sent their children north to families in small farming communities or to convents or monasteries in the hope that the children would be able to live through the war unharmed. Frieda, Elie, and I were usually not welcome in these places because people were afraid we would make noise, look out a window, or get sick and need a doctor. Suspicion and fear bred on each other in the cramped surroundings, and the atmosphere often bristled with tension. Mama instinctively knew when a house had become unsafe. She read the signs in the people around us. Many could not stand the pressures of hiding for a long period of time, and they would reveal the hiding place to an outsider. At one house the owner came home drunk one night, and Mama discovered that he had been boasting at the local bar that he was hiding Jews. There was always the fear that the people hiding us would turn us over to the Gestapo for a reward. As soon as Mama noticed any strange behavior, we contacted Kroll or Blanchka, gathered our belongings together, and sneaked out at night to go somewhere else.

One of the houses we stayed in was nicknamed the Devil's House. Thirty people were crowded into a crumbling old three-story building. We had a small room on the first floor. Individuals kept mostly to themselves, afraid of each other, and we stayed in our room unless we were using the bathroom or the kitchen. There was one pair of shoes which everyone shared. We had all run from hiding places so many times that no one had shoes any more. When one of us had to go outside to shop, to contact the Resistance, or to look for a lost loved one, he or she borrowed the shoes.

I had not thought to find a friend among the scarred and tortured souls we met. The few children that Kroll and Blanchka entrusted to Mama's care were taken to other places almost before we learned their names and heard their stories. But Anneke was different. At first when Kroll brought her to us, she cried uncontrollably. I watched Mama try to comfort her. She was my age, but smaller, with short dark hair that curled attractively around her face. Her arrival upset the other residents. They were afraid that her sobbing would be heard outside.

"Don't keep her," one of the men told my mother. "We can't have so much noise here."

"He's right," another agreed. "Send her back with your contact."

"Let me handle this," Mama said firmly, closing the door to our room.

She and Anneke sat on the bed while the girl wept steadily onto Mama's shoulder.

"Try to tell me about it, Anneke," Mama urged. But this only made her cry harder.

"Try," Mama insisted. "You'll feel better. You're safe here. You can talk to me."

Slowly, as she responded to Mama's tender manner, Anneke brought her sobbing under control and sat up, wiping her eyes with the backs of her hands. Little by little, Mama coaxed her to talk. Her story was like ours in many ways. I realized that, if circumstances had been different, I might have been in Anneke's place.

"We went into hiding two years ago, my mother and father, my brother Charles and I," she began, speaking slowly. "My parents had tried everything. Daddy even went into the hospital for an operation so that he wouldn't have to work on a German labor battalion. But the Gestapo raided the hospital. Luckily, a young doctor helped him escape through a basement door."

Mama nodded her head encouragingly. We knew that many sympathetic doctors had tried to save their friends and patients by surgically making them incapable of work.

"No one would help us," Anneke continued. "Mama even went to the Red Cross office where she had worked as a volunteer. Nothing. Daddy said we had to hide. He had a Christian friend who was being pressured by the Nazis to convert his business to the war effort. There had been threats that he and his family would be in danger if he didn't do what was asked. He refused. He was threatened with arrest. There was nowhere to run. He, too, had to hide."

Anneke stopped talking. She looked down at her hands folded in her lap and sighed deeply.

"You don't have to say any more," Mama said gently. "Let's get you something to eat before you do any more talking."

I went to the kitchen and came back with a cup of the soup that was simmering on the stove. Anneke drank gratefully. As soon as she was finished, she started talking again.

"My father and his friend worked out a plan," Anneke said. "We moved into the friend's house. His family lived in the basement with their cat. We lived on the main floor. The idea was that we would serve as decoys if the Gestapo came looking for him. We also whitewashed the windows, hoping that the house would look unoccupied and no one would bother us. The rumor was spread that my father's friend and his family had been taken away and that the house was empty. Only one neighbor knew what was happening. He supplied us with food."

Anneke's nose wrinkled in distaste as she mentioned food.

"Herring! Nothing but herring every day for two years! I never thought I could get so tired of eating fish."

We smiled. We were not strangers to any of this.

"We were so afraid of being caught that we didn't dare use the toilets in case someone would hear them being flushed. My job was to empty the chamberpots into the gutter early every morning before the neighbors were awake."

Anneke sighed again.

"My mother," she began. But these words started her tears flowing again, and she couldn't speak for a few minutes. Then she shook her head, as if she were forcing herself to face the truth, and continued.

"My mother was afraid that someone would turn us in to the Gestapo. She hid from the neighbor who delivered our food. As the months passed, she became more and more nervous. One morning I answered a knock on the back door, thinking it was the man who brought the fish. I was surprised to see a man dressed in a city worker's uniform standing there. He looked surprised to see me, too. 'I wasn't sure anyone was living here anymore,' he said, 'I'm here to read the gas meter.' When he left, my mother collapsed on the floor, clutching her chest and gasping for air.

"From that day on, my mother talked only of death. She was certain the gas man would report us to the authorities. She even suspected that he was spying for the Gestapo. My father promised to find another place for us to hide. Then one morning while I was emptying the chamberpots, I let the owner's cat out by mistake. Mother became hysterical. She screamed, 'Someone will see that cat! They'll know people are hiding here!' Again, she was overcome by horrible pain in her chest. There was nothing we could do. We had no doctor, no medicine."

Anneke's shoulders started heaving as she tried to tell us the rest. But Mama held her close, rocking to and fro and whispering, "It's all right, Anneke. It's all right."

"Why did she have to die?" Anneke sobbed. "She wasn't ready to die!"

Gradually, she stopped weeping. For a long time her breath came in short gasps, but, finally exhausted, Anneke fell asleep. She slept almost continuously for two days, waking to eat and to cry, until Mama calmed her and she drifted into slumber again. During the brief times that she was awake, she filled in the rest of her story.

After his wife died, Anneke's father again enlisted the help of friends. He sent her brother Charles to live on a farm north of Antwerp. She and her father were hidden in a beautiful home on Cardinale Mercier Boulevard that was owned by two middle-aged sisters. Anneke and her father felt that there was something odd about the women. They refused to talk about themselves and insisted on speaking French at all times. But, Anneke explained, she could tell from their accent that French was not their native language. When Anneke and her father lapsed into Flemish, the sisters didn't seem to understand them.

The sisters were extremely nervous, and, at first, Anneke

and her father assumed that it was because they were hiding Jews. They refused to let either Anneke or her father go out of the house for any reason. Anneke's father began to suspect that they were being trapped. He and Anneke made up a story that would convince the women that Anneke needed to see a doctor. Since the sisters would not consider allowing a doctor to visit the house, Anneke's father hoped that Anneke would be allowed out. Then she would try to contact the Resistance, which would help them find another place to stay. Their trick worked. Anneke left early one morning and contacted a Christian friend who lived on the Scheldt River.

"Something is wrong," she told him. "You have to help us get out of that house."

Soon after she returned to Cardinale Mercier Boulevard, there was a knock on the front door. Anneke and her father looked out the front window and saw a Gestapo truck parked in front of the house.

"Hide!" the sisters shouted. "Don't let them catch you!"

Anneke and her father stood at the window as though they were paralyzed.

"Run!" the women screamed. "They don't know about you. They have come for us."

In the bizarre scene that followed, Anneke and her father suddenly understood everything. The two women were German Jews. They themselves had been hiding from the Gestapo.

As Anneke and her father stood frozen in the living room, the soldiers broke down the door and, ignoring them, searched for the two women, finally trapping them in the kitchen. Anneke's father grabbed Anneke by the arm and propelled her out the door. They walked swiftly to the end of the street and looked back to see the women being carried into the army truck. Then they ran.

They hid in a church for two days. Anneke's father stole out at night to contact the Resistance. Kroll was assigned to help them. Anneke's father decided that Anneke would have a better chance of surviving without him. It was then that Kroll brought her to us at the Devil's House.

When Kroll came to see us a few days later, Mama told him that Anneke needed to be with her father.

"The child just sleeps and cries," Mama told him. "She's been through so much already. She is terrified to be alone."

"I'll see what I can do," Kroll promised.

True to his word, Kroll appeared the next day with Anneke's father. Almost instantly, Anneke stopped crying and began to take an interest in what was going on around her.

Anneke and I began to spend all our time together. We had both been without a friend for so long that we were hungry for companionship. Our favorite place to talk was the bottom step in the front hall. It was the most public place in the entire house, but in a house without privacy it seemed to lend a special air of seclusion we could not find in any of the crowded rooms. People came and went, passing by without taking any notice of us. We could stay there for hours, as though we were sitting outside our high-school building or on the steps of a library. We were like two schoolgirls sharing secrets and gossip, getting to know each other, forming a friendship that might last a lifetime.

We talked endlessly about the war, about ourselves, about what we remembered of life as it used to be and what it might be like in the uncertain future. Our talk was leisurely, for there was no homework or chores to do, no meetings or appointments to be kept, only the long hours of waiting to fill. Anneke told me that she admired Frieda because Frieda was brave enough to go out during the day. There was just one topic I learned to steer away from during our talks. Anneke felt that in some way the Jews must be the cause of their troubles, but she couldn't figure out what she had done to deserve everything that had happened to her.

"Look at me, Clara," she said in the middle of a

conversation. "The Nazis say we're ugly. Am I ugly?"

I smiled. "No," I replied, "I think you're beautiful."

"Then why do they say we're all ugly? Do you remember the posters and the cartoons in the newspapers before we went into hiding?"

"Yes, I remember," I said, thinking about how Mama had made fun of Nazi propaganda. "You mustn't believe that sort of thing, Anneke."

But she wasn't convinced, and I learned to avoid the subject.

Those weeks that Anneke lived at the Devil's House were the happiest I had known in hiding. She was despondent at times, and as tearful over her mother's death as I was over Daddy's. But we had so much to share that the time passed easily. Her brother Charles, however, was terribly lonely and wanted his sister and father to join him. Anneke was torn, but finally decided to go to her brother. Her father chose to stay at the Devil's House. He had lived for so long without people to talk to that, as long as he knew his children were safe, he preferred to stay with us. Anneke had been with us only three weeks when, amid tearful good-bys, Kroll took her to the farm where her brother was hiding.

Then, just as I was becoming accustomed to the loneliness again, Anneke appeared one evening, exhausted, to try to convince her father to join her and Charles at the farm.

"How did you get back here?" Mama asked her, realizing that Kroll hadn't brought her.

"I couldn't reason with my brother, Mrs. Heller. He insisted that we must all be together. So I begged and begged the farmer to bring me back. And, oh, Mrs. Heller, it was awful! I couldn't find the house! We walked for hours and hours!"

Anneke knew what street the Devil's House was on. She was sure she even knew which block, but she didn't remember the exact address. However, she did remember a green door, and early the previous evening she and the farmer had come to the city. But there was no green door. They walked up and down for more than an hour searching for a clue that would help them identify the house. As curfew time approached the farmer became frightened. They must not be seen wandering aimlessly on the street. But Anneke insisted they were in the right place. They must have missed the door. They continued to walk up and down the street where we were hiding and up and down the neighboring streets. Anneke was almost hysterical in her helplessness, the farmer terrified that they would be stopped by an army patrol. It was well after midnight when they finally gave up their search. But Anneke would not go back to the farm. She knew how to find Kroll, who let them stay with him overnight. The following evening Kroll brought them to the Devil's House. They had walked past the house again and again the night before, but the door they were looking for was green only on the inside. Outside it was white.

As Anneke's father prepared to leave with Anneke and Kroll, we said our good-bys once more.

"Will I ever see you again, Clara?" Anneke asked, almost in tears.

"Oh, I hope so!" I cried, holding her close. "Kroll will bring us news of each other, and when the war is over we'll be friends forever."

I hoped I sounded more certain than I felt. The Nazis had destroyed so much of both our lives, I couldn't let them destroy our hopes as well.

13 · On Stadion Street

January 1945

The days that followed Anneke's departure were empty. Our family drew even closer together, but there was little comfort in Mama's "Just a little bit longer, children, I'm sure it will be just a little bit longer."

It seemed as though the war would never end. The Devil's House appeared to grow smaller as more people, homeless and wretched, were brought to live there. The fear of collaborators was always with us, and we were suspicious of every newcomer. Squabbles broke out over petty matters, the distribution of food, or the use of the bathroom. Mama talked to Kroll about moving again, but safe houses in Antwerp were increasingly hard to find. With each new spurt of Gestapo activity there were fewer people willing to hide Jews.

Mama, Kroll and Blanchka developed a plan. Blanchka borrowed clothes and shoes for Frieda. Posing as Kroll's wife, Frieda went with him to rent a house. The Resistance

had had some success renting empty houses for Jews disguised
as gentiles, and Kroll was willing to be part of the deception.
They told the rental agent that Frieda's mother would also be
living with them, but that she was mute, struck speechless by
disease several years before. They did not mention me or
Elie.

The ruse worked. They rented a little house on Stadion
Street. It was just a block away from the stadium where the
German soldiers held their sporting events. Frieda, Kroll,
and Mama made a big show of moving in one afternoon. Elie
and I were brought in secretly after dark that night. It was a
daring plan, but one that Kroll felt would work. The tide had
turned against Germany on several fronts, and Kroll was
convinced the Nazis would now spend less time and effort
rounding up the few remaining Jews.

I thought the house was pretty, even though it had not
been cared for. There was furniture in each of the rooms.
There was even a piano in the living room that we were not
allowed to play, lest it attract the attention of the neighbors.
How difficult it was for Frieda to be deprived of her precious
music with that piano nearby! Behind the kitchen was a small
garden surrounded by a high wall. Elie and I could sit out
there at night, look up at the stars, and breathe in the cool
night air—something we hadn't done in almost two years.

To complete her image as a Christian housewife, Frieda
had her hair dyed blonde at a beauty parlor across the street
and replaced the Star of David around her neck with a golden
cross. She carried the Star of David in her shoe. In this
disguise, she felt more confident than ever outside the house.
Mama still worried when Frieda went out, but she understood that Frieda was making her own contribution to the
Resistance effort and didn't try to stop her.

Almost every weekend we heard cars jockeying for
parking places and the gay chatter of the crowd as it passed
our curtained windows on the way to the stadium. It was still
hard for me to realize that there were people in Antwerp

leading normal lives, going to school or to work, having fun on weekends. Most of Antwerp had no idea that people were living behind closed doors and painted windows.

One night, Kroll took me for a walk in the empty stadium. The evening air, blowing coolly through the empty stands, was sweeter than I remembered. We walked slowly around the athletes' track, Kroll letting me drink in every detail of the moonlit scene: the geraniums in the private boxes, the flags and statues at the entrance. I pictured the stands filled with people, the contestants warming up on the grass inside the track. I heard the cheers as the runners rounded the turn nearest the crowd, and saw their breathless faces at the finishing line.

"Do you think I'll ever come here in daylight?" I whispered to Kroll.

"Of course you will," he said softly. "It can't be much longer now."

When Kroll felt that we were well established on Stadion Street, that the neighbors were not overly curious about him and Frieda and Mama, he started secretly bringing other wanderers to live with us. Sometimes Frieda accompanied him on his rounds of hiding places. One day she returned with a frightened little girl no more than four years old who had been hidden with gentiles. Because many non-Jews had been imprisoned for housing Jewish children, the Resistance now worked to move as many children as it could to safer places. We knew the child would be with us only until Kroll could find a better place for her, probably outside the city. She was thin and pretty, with curly blonde hair and huge, trusting brown eyes. Mama's face lit up when she held the child on her lap, singing to her and combing her curls. Will I ever have a child of my own to sing to, I wondered. Will there be any Jews left to create a new generation? When Kroll took the child away a few days later, a measure of our hope seemed to leave with her.

Blanchka brought us an old Jewish gentleman whom she

had found wandering in the street. It was after dark, almost time for curfew, when she noticed him standing at a busy intersection. He looked confused, pointing his cane first one way and then another, as though he was trying to decide which direction he had come from.

"Can I help you, Grandfather?" she asked in Yiddish. "Where do you live? I'll take you home."

"Eh?" The old man groaned, startled and staring at her through watery eyes.

"Where do you live?" Blanchka repeated, glancing nervously over her shoulder to make sure they were not overheard.

He mentioned an address on one of the streets that the Nazis had cleared of Jews many months before. Clearly, he had been hidden somewhere, but he could not remember where or with whom. His mind was playing the trick of old age. He saw events and places of long ago in sharp detail and forgot what had happened a few hours before.

"I just came out for a little walk," he said. "It's very embarrassing, you know, but I'm afraid I've lost my way."

"It's all right, Grandfather, I'll take you home. Come with me."

Blanchka crooked her arm through his and the old man leaned on her gratefully. They walked slowly, the old man jabbing his cane at sticks and leaves in their path and pushing them aside. Blanchka's mind was racing. Where could she take him? They were not very far from Stadion Street. Mrs. Heller would surely take him in, she thought, if only they could get there before they were spotted by a Nazi patrol.

"*A gezhunt oyf dein haartz*," the old man said over and over, blessing Blanchka's good heart for helping him.

If only he would walk a little faster, Blanchka thought, I'd bless his heart, too.

The faces that greeted us as we answered Blanchka's urgent knock were almost comical in contrast. Blanchka was so relieved to have gotten him safely to the house that she didn't know whether to laugh or cry. The old gentleman stood in the doorway baffled, suddenly aware that Blanchka had not taken him to the home he remembered.

In a few moments Mama had them settled on the sofa and was serving bread and tea out of our scanty provisions while we listened to Blanchka. She was relaxed now and laughed at the absurdity of her experience.

Of course we would take care of the gentleman, Mama said. It would be no trouble at all. Frieda and I would give him our room. Blanchka turned to the man and explained what was happening. He seemed to understand, for he kept patting her hand and repeating, "*A gezhunt oyf dein haartz, a gezhunt oyf dein haartz.*"

His name was Jacob Krauss. He seemed happy to be with us. For the next few weeks he moved quietly about the house or sat in a chair in the living room, dozing and daydreaming. He wanted to be helpful, and insisted on cleaning up after meals, carefully washing and drying each dish until he was satisfied it was spotless. Sometimes he became confused, and one of us would show him to his bedroom or the bathroom.

His happiness would be complete, Mr. Krauss said, if we would let him go for his afternoon walk. His legs needed the exercise, he insisted. We had to explain repeatedly why we couldn't let him go. He seemed to understand, but the next day we would have to explain it all over again. One afternoon when no one was looking he opened the front door and walked outside. Mama was extremely upset when we discovered he was gone. Frieda was out with Kroll, the neighbors had been told that Mama was mute, and they didn't even know that Elie and I existed. But there was no choice.

"Clara, you'll have to go and find him," Mama said.

I dashed out the door. He hadn't gotten very far. When I caught up with him on the next street he beamed at me, his dim eyes laughing behind his glasses.

"I'm having a nice walk, my dear," he announced like a little boy who has been caught with a fist full of candy. "It's a lovely afternoon."

"Yes, I know, Mr. Krauss," I replied, gently turning him back toward the house. "But Mama was worried about you."

"Why should she worry? I can find my way."

"Of course you can," I agreed. "But it's getting late now. It's time to go home."

We made our way back to the house slowly, arm in arm. He talked about the beautiful weather, the flowers in the neat little gardens we passed, and the faces of the children he had seen. Poor dear old man, I mused. But perhaps he's happier being unaware of the danger we're all in, I thought. The world he is living in is at peace.

But one day, in spite of all our care, Mr. Krauss walked out of the house and melted into the streets of Antwerp. We never saw him or heard about him again. I searched the neighborhood, but I couldn't ask anyone if he had been seen. Certainly a woman scrubbing her front step or a delivery man or a shopkeeper might have been able to help me. But they also might have been suspicious and reported us to the Gestapo. I had loved caring for the old man and missed him when he was gone.

More than anything during the endless months of 1944 we needed to hear what was happening to other people in hiding. Kroll, reticent by nature, told us very little. We knew he felt deeply, but his emotions lay buried under a businesslike façade. Sometimes, in just a sentence or two, he would tell us about something he had done or seen. He told us about an important Jewish man who was hiding in the back room of a grocery store. Kroll received word that the Gestapo knew the man's whereabouts. He carried the man out of the store in a sack like a load of potatoes only minutes before the Gestapo arrived.

"I brought bread, jam, and milk to a man hiding in a basement," Kroll told us another time. "He ate in a great hurry, not even thanking me until everything was finished. 'I just ate a feast, a feast fit for a king,' he said. 'For the last three weeks I have eaten only enough to feed a bird.'

Mama and Daddy had always practiced tzedakah—charity—when we lived on Leeuwerick Street. Two alms boxes sat on a shelf in our kitchen: one for Jews in Palestine, the other for Jewish widows and orphans. Each Friday afternoon, before lighting the Sabbath candles, Mama dropped coins into the boxes. Their *plunk, plunk* was part of the sounds and sights and smells that I associated with the Sabbath. Mama never stopped practicing tzedakah, even in hiding. Wherever we were hidden, there was always room for one more. She was never too tired or too upset to listen to someone else's problems. So the little house on Stadion Street became a gathering place for other homeless people. Resistance workers came, at first to make us feel better, but they kept returning because Mrs. Heller was such good company.

Passover arrived. We remembered how we had prayed for freedom and an end to the war at Mrs. Brussels's house. It was discouraging to realize that we had been hiding for almost two years, that we were still in danger, that there was no end in sight. Then, by some miracle, Kroll appeared with a box of matzo and a chicken, all plucked and quartered. We could hardly contain our excitement.

"Where did you get a chicken, Kroll?" Mama exclaimed. "I can't remember the last time we had a chicken. And matzo!"

"Now we can really celebrate Pesach," I said.

"I thought you'd be pleased," Kroll told Mama.

Mama was silent for a while.

"Kroll," she said, "will you do a favor for me?"

"If I can, I'll be happy to."

"I'm sure you can. Go to Rabbi Niederman. Take Clara with you. I want him to have the chicken and the matzo. He'll enjoy it."

"But, but it's for you."

"I know, Kroll, but I couldn't enjoy it if I knew I was eating a chicken and the rabbi wasn't. Please, this will make me even happier."

With a shrug of his shoulders, Kroll rewrapped the chicken in its newspaper and told me to get ready.

Rabbi Niederman was living in one room in the basement of an apartment building. Kroll drove to the neighborhood and parked the car on an adjacent street. We proceeded on foot, making sure we weren't being followed.

The rabbi was huddled in a huge easy chair which sprouted tufts of stuffing here and there. His legs were covered with blankets. Surrounding him on all sides were stacks of books that he had somehow managed to bring into hiding. He was reading by the light of a dim lamp. As we entered, his blue eyes blinked as he tried to focus on Kroll and me.

"*Shalom*, Rabbi Niederman," I said, moving in front of his chair so he could see me more clearly. "I am Clara Heller. Perhaps you remember my family."

He did remember and wanted to know everything that had happened to us since the occupation. As he sat listening, I thought he looked as old and worn and frayed as the chair he was sitting in.

"Rabbi," Kroll said, "Mrs. Heller has sent you a chicken and some matzo for the Passover holiday."

The old man shook his head and brushed at his eyes.

"Tell Mrs. Heller thank you very much. I will be happy to accept the matzo; she is most kind. But please, take the chicken back with you. There are many of you, Clara, and you will enjoy such a treat."

"Mama specifically said that you were to have it," I insisted. "She would be angry if we did not complete our errand."

The good man tried another argument.

"It is Shabbat, my dear. You know I cannot light the oven today. By the time Shabbat is over, the chicken will start to spoil."

I listened and nodded as he spoke, thinking of a way of getting around the rabbi's stubborn generosity. I made a sign to Kroll to distract the rabbi while I sidled into the alcove that served as a kitchen and lit the oven with a match. I knew that, despite his protestations, the rabbi would be grateful for the chicken. Finding a pan, I checked the bird for pin feathers and, finding none, put it in the oven. Kroll and I chatted with the rabbi for a few more minutes, until the smell of roasting chicken made our mouths water.

As I left the rabbi's little room, I remembered the dear face of my beloved Daddy. I remembered all the Hebrew books we had had in our house, the seders we celebrated.

"Is he safe there alone?" I asked Kroll on the ride home.

"I hope so," he replied.

Spring arrived, and I could peek through the curtains in the living room and see the roses blooming in the little garden in front of the house. The days grew longer, and we looked at the daylight with mixed emotions. The bright sky lifted our spirits, but the light also made us easier to see. We had to be more careful.

In the back of the house there was a small porch which could not be seen from the street. Mama was resting there one sultry afternoon when a child's ball bounced over the wall and landed on the step just below where she was sitting. Without thinking, Mama picked the ball up and threw it back over the wall. She came inside, shaking, wondering whether it had been a mistake to throw it back. It would have been far more dangerous, we reasoned, if the child had climbed the wall to retrieve the ball and discovered a house full of refugees. From then on, even the little porch was off-limits during the day.

On Stadion Street we were able to receive a more varied assortment of guests than in any of the other places in hiding. There was von Oste, Blanchka's husband, who was a colonel in the Belgian army. He worked for the Germans during the day and for the Resistance at night. During the few times he visited us, he told us stories. He was always walking a tightrope, gathering information during the day about Gestapo raids and policies, and using that knowledge at night, rescuing the Jews for whom the Germans had set their trap.

He wasn't always successful, and there were nights when he sat despondently on our couch grieving over those he had failed to reach soon enough. Because von Oste worked with German officialdom, he was sometimes invited to meetings and conferences. One evening he told us he had dined at an estate in the country with a handful of German military brass. He thought the maid who was waiting on tables looked familiar. He was able to draw her aside after the meal long enough to find out that she was, indeed, Anaka, my friend from the Devil's House.

She sent us greetings and the message that she, her father, and brother were all fine. She had taken a position as a chambermaid on an ancient estate used by German officers. She listened carefully to their conversations when she could, and reported to her Resistance contact everything she learned. I was ecstatic to hear that she was alive and well, and more than a little jealous that she was actively helping the Resistance.

$$14 \cdot \textit{A breath of air}$$

April 1945

The longer we stayed on Stadion Street, the more we learned about what was happening in Antwerp. Our house became a regular resting place for a few Resistance workers. They knew they had to be consistent in their movements because many of them were under observation by the Gestapo, which watched for any suspicious change in their activities. We looked forward to their visits and became anxious when someone didn't appear at the expected time. Once, a Resistance worker visited us when he was in great danger, but a change in his routine would have spelled even greater danger for himself and others, including us. This was Joseph Sterngold, who became one of Mama's closest friends in hiding.

One night Mr. Sterngold came to us pale and shaken. He needed Mama's comfort and advice. He sat at the table in the kitchen, wracked with guilt.

"How could I have been so stupid?" he wondered aloud.

"I never leave lists lying around. How did they know I lived there? How can I go back?"

"You're not making sense, Joseph," Mama said. "Tell me what happened. Start at the beginning."

"I had a new list, one I had not yet memorized. It was a list of names and addresses of people in hiding whom I had been assigned to contact. Perhaps a hundred people! A hundred human beings!"

The poor man cradled his head in his hands and rocked to and fro. Mama rose from her chair and went over to him, placing a comforting arm around his shoulders.

"You can't do this to yourself, Joseph," she insisted. "How do you know the Gestapo has the list?"

"When I realized I had forgotten it, I went back to my room. The Gestapo must have seen me leave. They're fast workers. I couldn't have been gone more than fifteen minutes. When I got there, the room had been completely torn apart. The list was gone. Why didn't they wait for me and pick me up?"

"You're more valuable to them this way," Mama said. She spoke coldly, matter-of-factly, but we all knew she was telling the truth. "They'd rather use you as a pipeline for information. They won't dispose of you until you've outlived your usefulness. How did you get into this unprofitable line of work?" Mama asked, trying to steer the conversation away from Mr. Sterngold's immediate worry.

Mr. Sterngold lifted his head and looked at Mama for a long moment, then at the three of us. I noticed how blue his eyes were under his bushy brown eyebrows and wondered whether those eyes made it easier for him to walk around Antwerp these days. He shrugged his shoulders and leaned back in his chair, lighting one of the cigarettes Mama offered him. Inhaling deeply, he closed his eyes for a moment, blew the smoke upward into the circle of yellow lamplight, and started telling us his story.

"I escaped from the Dannes-Camiers work camp in

Boulogne in September nineteen forty-two," he said. "I'll spare you the horrors of that place. I was there only a month, but that was enough. When men were no longer healthy enough to work, they were taken to another camp called Auschwitz. I was determined not to let that happen to me.

"When I got back to Antwerp I found that my entire family—my mother, brother, and two sisters—had been deported. I started searching for other people I knew. I was probably in a state of shock as I dialed one telephone number after another and never reached anyone. I visited streets all over the city where my friends and acquaintances had lived. It was as though some horrible plague had descended on everyone I knew and made them disappear. Finally, I found the wife of a friend. Her husband had also been taken to a work camp in northern France. This woman introduced me to the Resistance. She gave me something to do and a reason to go on living. That's why I'm so upset. I know better than to be careless. I know what those people will be going through."

"We are all doing the best we can, Joseph," Mama said soothingly. "We are only human."

"But what we're fighting is inhuman!"

Mama said nothing. She kept still and waited to change the subject again. "Where were you last week, Joseph? I was worried when you didn't come."

The blue eyes smiled at Mama as if to say Mr. Sterngold was grateful there was someone who thought and worried about him.

"I was off on a little trip to the mountains," he began, the teasing lilt that we were accustomed to returning around the edges of his voice. "We knew about a very sick child in a little village in the Ardennes. The child needed medicine, but we could not get a Belgian doctor to visit her. It's too dangerous for them to care for Jews anymore, even in the small villages. A messenger told us what was needed, and I set off on the train. The child's mother was told to wait at the station. I would only have to walk past her and hand her the medicine. It was a routine procedure unless someone stopped me for questioning. If that happened, I had the means to make certain I would not reveal anything."

He would have taken his life. He talked so casually about his own death, I thought, and so passionately about preventing the deaths of others. My respect for Mr. Sterngold deepened as he continued speaking.

"I delivered the medicine without incident, pretending to get off the train in search of a cup of coffee. The woman was waiting in the shadows cast by the overhanging roof of the little station house. She had wrapped a white scarf around her neck. That was the signal I had been told to look for. She appeared to be checking the train schedule nailed to the wall, but after I brushed by her, handing her the medicine, she quickly disappeared."

Mr. Sterngold was beginning to enjoy recounting this adventure to the attentive little group around the table. Elie had not stirred. Frieda and I nodded, urging our guest to continue as he took a sip of the coffee Mama had placed in front of him.

"This village was at the end of the line. Here the trains reverse for the return trip. I reboarded the train and returned to my seat. Then I noticed two soldiers making their way through the railroad car. They were checking the passengers' papers in that methodically officious way they have, making sure that everyone had the proper identification for that section of the country."

Since June 1943, men between the ages of eighteen and thirty-five had to carry a work card with them at all times that described the area and the type of work they were assigned to. There were rules that prevented people from traveling outside the district where they were assigned to work.

"I hadn't had time to get false papers for that area," Mr. Sterngold continued, "so I had to think of something before those soldiers got to my seat. Luckily, the train had not started moving. I assumed that the soldiers had to complete their inspection and leave the train before it pulled out of the station. I glanced out the window and noticed that the station office was open. Clutching my stomach, I left the train, this time pretending I had to find a bathroom. There were three soldiers in the waiting room, but they paid no attention to me. I stayed in the men's room until I heard the conductor shout 'All aboard' and I heard the sounds of the train getting under way. I raced out of the lavatory and through the station. The inspectors were at the opposite end of the platform looking at their papers. I jumped onto the train just as it started to pick up speed."

"Whew, what luck!" Elie breathed.

We all nodded. It was more than luck, I thought to myself. It was good thinking that saved him, just as Mama's good judgment guided us through the maze of hiding places during the past two years.

We had a little radio which we kept hidden under a table. After April 18, 1944, it was illegal for Belgians to own and operate radios, so we were especially careful to make sure our neighbors could not hear us using it. It was a lifeline, a link to the outside world. It stayed under a table in the living room, hidden by a huge tablecloth that fell to the floor. We took turns lying underneath the cloth and listening. Our hopes rose and fell as the seesaw of the war's progress continued. Each night at six o'clock we tried to tune our radio to the BBC, the British Broadcasting Company. In June we heard that Rome had fallen to the Allies. On June 6 the Allies landed at Normandy. The Americans were on European soil! We were certain that the war could not last much longer. On July 20 we listened, amazed, to reports that there had been an attempt to kill Hitler. There were people in Germany, too, who wanted the madness to end.

Just as our hopes were beginning to rise, a face from our past sent us into a tailspin. One afternoon in late July, Kroll brought a young man named Dror Pritchik to see us. I had known him slightly as the leader of a Jewish youth group. He was Heshie's age, about eighteen years old. At the start of the occupation he had organized a group of thirteen and fourteen year olds from his youth group to travel through France to freedom in Switzerland. They had been captured near the Swiss border. The Nazis sent Dror to a work camp. He escaped and started working with the Resistance, only to be captured twice more and sent to other camps. He had a wild, restless look that I did not remember from happier times. But Kroll had not brought him to us to reminisce.

"Let's all sit down," Kroll said after we had greeted each other. "Dror has something to tell you."

"It's about Heshie, isn't it?" Mama asked as she sat nervously on the edge of a chair.

Dror nodded his head reluctantly, obviously upset by what he had to tell us.

"He's dead," Mama said before Dror could speak.

Mama rocked back and forth in her chair, clutching her sides like a person in pain.

"Kroll wanted you to hear it in person," Dror said earnestly. "You should be very proud of what Heshie did."

We had all but given up hope that Heshie was still alive. It had been more than two years since he had gone away, and all we had received was one tattered postcard soon after he left. Speaking softly, Dror pieced together what he knew and what he had learned about Heshie.

"Heshie was sent to work on the wall the Germans were building along the French coast. The boys worked twelve and sixteen hours a day, laying barbed wire, building concrete bunkers. The food was poor, and they were exposed to every sort of weather. They slept in tents. When they got sick or hurt they were shipped east to one of the concentration camps to do other kinds of work. Heshie was one of the stronger boys, but, eventually, he became sick, probably with pneumonia. They told Heshie they were going to send him somewhere to recover. But that was a lie. They took him to Auschwitz, a death camp."

Dror's voice had dropped so low we could barely make out his words. He paused, not knowing whether we could bear to hear more.

"Go on, Dror," Mama urged. "We must know everything."

"Even though he was weakened by his illness, Heshie was good at whatever the Nazis set him to do. In time they offered him the position of *kapo*."

Dror saw the questioning look on our faces. We had never heard that term.

"A *kapo* is a privileged prisoner. He's given extra rations or warm clothing in return for doing special jobs for the guards."

"What kind of jobs?" Elie asked.

"Anything that's too distasteful for the guards to do, Elie. The other prisoners consider *kapos* traitors. But let me tell you right away that Heshie refused to become one of them."

Mama nodded silently, her suffering written on her face. It had been hard not to know whether Heshie was alive or not, but discovering that he died in that awful place was somehow worse than not knowing and hoping.

"Heshie died soon after he refused to become a *kapo*. Everyone respected him for his decision. Everyone loved him."

We were all sobbing when Dror finished. We never saw him leave. He recognized that we needed to be alone, to absorb the shock of Heshie's death. There really is no going back, I thought. Nothing will ever be the same.

The war was coming to a close in our corner of the world. It was late summer, and each day brought new reports of Allied gains. For a while, even after the tide had turned against them, the German army continued to round up Jews. But by the end of August 1944 even that horrible effort had stopped. Kroll told us that the Nazis who had been in charge of running the occupation were leaving Antwerp in great numbers, scurrying back to Germany for safety.

We listened to the Allies' progress on the radio. It was true! Antwerp would soon be liberated by the Allies.

One night, Colonel von Oste came to our house with Blanchka. "George has something to tell you," she said.

"Antwerp is going to be liberated in just a few hours," he told us. "But I want you all to stay here, do you hear me? Stay here. I know that you will want to go out, but it will be very dangerous. That's why I took the chance of coming here—to convince you that your lives will be in danger if you go out during the first few hours after liberation."

We looked at von Oste in amazement. I was confused. Didn't liberation mean freedom?

"It will not be safe for any strangers to be on the streets. You are to wait here until Blanchka or I tell you it's safe."

What I hadn't considered was the suffering of all the Antwerp citizens, whether in hiding or not. As the Allies entered our city, many of its townspeople did indeed go on a rampage against those who had sided with the Germans. People were in the street waving American and British flags. There was singing and shouting. One of the women in a neighboring house had been friendly with Nazi soldiers. She was dragged out of her house by an angry mob, who shaved off her hair and then forced her onto the back of a truck. They drove down the street while other neighbors jeered and threw things at her.

We were so absorbed in watching this spectacle that we didn't notice a man emerge from next door holding a huge German shepherd on a leash. I answered his angry knock. Bursting into the living room, he pointed a shotgun at us and said, "All right, I know who you are. Get outdoors where everyone can see you."

"What are you talking about?" Mama demanded, no longer the cautious woman in hiding.

"We know you're hiding Germans in here. We could hear your radio every night."

"Oh, my God," Mama said. "We're Jews!" And she began to laugh a deep-throated laugh.

Just then Blanchka came in the door. It must have been a strange scene: Mama laughing, the stranger with the menacing-looking dog and the shotgun, we children open-mouthed and staring.

Shortly the awful misunderstanding was ironed out. We had suspected our neighbors of being German sympathizers when, in truth, they had been working for the Resistance and were equally suspicious of us.

"Come," Blanchka said, "it's time to go outside."

The sun was shining fiercely in the heat of late summer as our little group walked wearily outside. There was no exultation, no dancing and singing. We had lost too much. But there was a quiet joy in knowing that the worst was over. I leaned against the doorpost feeling faint in the sunlight.

Dear Daddy, dear Heshie, I thought, dear friends and neighbors whom I have lost, I will try to make my life worthy of your memory. You will always be with me. I felt a faint, warm breeze and, for the first time in many months, took a deep, full . . . free . . . breath of air.

Epilogue

Most of my friends mentioned in this book died in concentration camps or were caught by the Gestapo while they were running from one hiding place to another. Pita, one of my leaders from Hashomer Hatzair, survived and is living on a kibbutz in Israel. Batya is now a nurse in a hospital in Beersheba, Israel. We had a joyously tearful reunion in the summer of 1956. My mother is eighty-five years old and lives in her own apartment in New York City, still giving her children the benefit of her advice. My sister Frieda has two sons, a daughter, and a grandson. My brother Elie has two daughters and a son. Mr. Yeager, Blanchka, and von Oste still live in Antwerp. We keep in touch regularly. Until 1979, I was not certain whether Anneke survived. Today, we are close friends once more. She has a successful business in Antwerp and two lovely daughters. Anneke's brother Charles also survived. He married a daughter of one of the families that helped save his life.